The Amazing Adventures of
THE ESCAPIST™

VOLUME 3

Based on
The Amazing Adventures of Kavalier & Clay
by Michael Chabon

Cover Art by Tim Sale

DARK HORSE BOOKS™

CONTENTS

CONTENTS

WILL EISNER

March 6, 1917 – January 3, 2005

Will Eisner did *not* want to do this story.

Really. I caught him in a moment of weakness and then wouldn't let him forget it. I am, as Will once called me, a "demon editor."

At the time, my editorial projects included (among others) this book and *A Spirited Life*, the authorized biography of Will Eisner written by Bob Andelman. Bob and Will were hoping that Michael Chabon would write an introduction to the biography; Michael was hoping that Will would write and draw a story for this comic in which the Spirit meets the Escapist.

So I struck a deal, negotiated a little trade. From my perspective as then-editor of both projects, it was a win-win scenario.

In the five years that I was blessed to be Will's Dark Horse editor, I grew to love the man — over and above my respect for him as the comics legend. Despite his overwhelming accomplishments, Will had a knack for always making you feel special. Will Eisner: comics entrepreneur and creator of *The Spirit;* pioneer of creators' rights, in an era when that was considered a preposterous notion; creator and promoter of educational comics; graphic novelist whose first, *A Contract with God,* was published decades before the format became so popular; educator and writer of *Comics & Sequential Art,* the field's seminal textbook; the man after whom our industry awards are named — *Will Eisner* made *you* feel special.

Damn, I miss him.

Will used to joke that he could never refuse me anything. But asking Will to return to a character whom he'd left behind in 1952 — to, eventually, pursue stories set in the real world, about real people and their real hopes and dreams, stories that were far more personally meaningful to Will than the pursuit-and-vengeance standard of most adventure tales — that required some *serious* sweet-talking.

But once Will agreed to something, he never backed down. He sure took his time, though, about doing this story — and I knew his heart wasn't really in it. Finally, I recommended that he just ditch the usual superhero conventions altogether and write a story about these two guys, Denny Colt and Tom Mayflower, who actually have a lot in common, right down to the mask (that Will always hated putting on the Spirit, by the way).

The non-genre approach piqued Will's interest — and then he did me one better, by working that approach into an adventure story, after all!

God bless him, he was so good.

The day after Will sent me these finished pages, he went into the hospital. He died there two and a half weeks later, and my heart broke.

It is both fitting and ironic that this should be Will's last work. Ironic, because he'd moved so far beyond the genre conventions of *The Spirit,* and while he was proud of the innovations he'd created all those years ago, he felt his graphic novels were more important, more literary, more a testament to what comics could — and should — really be.

Yet it is absolutely fitting that Will should have come full circle and left us with this one last Spirit story, a final gift to all his readers and fans who clamored for half a century for just this.

That should make all of us feel very special.

Diana Schutz

BY M.CHABON
THE SPIRIT
BY WILL EISNER
HEY... KAVALIER, DID OUR BOOK GET HERE YET?
NOT YET, CLAY! THE PRINTER SENT THE BOOK BY COURIER BECAUSE IT IS SO VALUABLE!
YEAH! IT'LL BE WORTH A FORTUNE IN A COUPLE OF YEARS!
SURE, LOOK HOW MUCH SUPERMAN NUMBER ONE SOLD FOR AT AUCTION!

WAIT! NOT THAT WAY, COURIER!
IT'S AN AMBUSH!

WH-- WHERE AM I ??
MY MEN OVERWHELMED YOU...SADLY, THEY KILLED THE POOR COURIER!
SPIRIT, DEAR...I HAVE YOU AT LAST!! WHERE IS THE FIRST EDITION THAT THE COURIER GAVE YOU AS HE LAY DYING??
IT'S P'GELL ...OH, BOY! ...OH, BOY!
I ATE IT, P'GELL!
VERY FUNNY, DARLING!
WELL, DEAR BOY, AFTER A LONG AND PAINFUL IMPRISONMENT AND A LITTLE TORTURE BY MY COLLEAGUES, ...YOU'LL GIVE IT UP...BYE-BYE...

GRRR!!!
UUGH!!
...CAN'T FREE MYSELF!
WHO IS THIS?
I'M THE ESCAPIST!
I'VE HEARD OF YOU...SO WHAT ARE YOU DOING HERE?
I'M ALSO P'GELL'S PRISONER, PIRIT! SHE'S TRYING TO GET HABON TO PAY A RANSOM FOR ME...HUMILIATING!
IT'S JUST AS EMBARRASSING FOR ME...UGH, I CAN'T GET OUT OF THESE ROPES!

OH... THEY'RE EASILY LOOSENED, SPIRIT! FOLLOW MY INSTRUCTIONS ...IT'S AN OLD HOUDINI TRICK. YOU'LL BE OUT IN A JIFFY!
OKAY!
IT WORKED! I'M **FREE**... NOW, LET'S SEE IF I CAN HELP FREE **YOU**!
HMM...WHAT IS THIS... A STEEL BINDING?
IT'S AN ELECTRONIC DEVICE! I CAN'T FIGURE OUT HOW IT WORKS!
...THERE NOW!
THANKS, SPIRIT! BUT PLEASE DON'T TELL ANYONE ABOUT THIS! ...**ESCAPING** IS MY **SPECIALTY**, Y'SEE!
YOU CAN COUNT ON IT... AND I WAS **SAVED BY A SUPERHERO**!!! WOW, **EISNER** WILL HAVE AN ULCER IF HE EVER HEARS ABOUT IT!

TELL ME, ESCAPIST, HAVE YOU EVER WONDERED WHAT HEROES DO FOR SOCIETY?
...DON'T HAVE MUCH TIME TO DWELL ON "WHY"! ...BUT I GUESS WHAT WE GIVE ARE... INSTANT SOLUTIONS AND HAPPY ENDINGS!
SOCIETY JUST WANTS TO WATCH US DO IT AGAIN AND AGAIN! EH, SPIRIT?
OH... WAIT!
HERE, GIVE THIS TO KAVALIER AND CLAY!
WHEW... THE FIRST EDITION OF THEIR BOOK... NOW, THAT IS A HAPPY ENDING!

THE DEATH OF THE ESCAPIST

QUOD CITY, CAPITAL OF THE REPUBLIC OF QUODESIA.
CENTURIES AGO, BRITISH COLONISTS CALLED THIS LAND "QUOD"-- OR "PRISON"-- FOR ITS VIRTUALLY IMPENETRABLE GEOGRAPHY...
... BUT THEY COULDN'T HAVE GUESSED JUST HOW APPROPRIATE THAT NAME WOULD EVENTUALLY PROVE TO BE.
STAND ASIDE. THE GREAT LEADER IS EXPECTING ME.
... CONCERNED ABOUT RECENT REPORTS OF ANTI-REGIME-- WHO DARES?!
GREAT LEADER SURELY REMEMBERS... THE SOLDIER HE SUMMONED TO HIS OFFICE?

OH? OF COURSE!
FOOL! GIVE THIS TO ME!
HOW DOES THIS-- THIS PROPAGANDA FIND ITS WAY INTO MY COUNTRY?
ESCAPIST
YOU! DID YOU READ ANY OF THIS BEFORE BRINGING IT HERE?
THE ESCAPIST
N-NEVER! I KNOW SUCH THINGS ARE FORBIDDEN!
"THE ESCAPIST"-- BAH!
THE VERY IDEA IS DANGEROUS. EVEN IN SOMETHING AS INSIPID AS THIS-- THIS COMIC BOOK!
WHAP!
I AM THE ONLY HOPE, THE ONLY HERO THE PEOPLE OF QUODESIA NEED. PERHAPS I NEED TO REMIND THEM.
PERHAPS I SHOULD CRUSH THIS ESCAPIST, JUST AS I HAVE CRUSHED HIS POISONOUS PAMPHLET. THEN THE PEOPLE WILL ABANDON ANY DREAMS OF "ESCAPING."

LEAVE ME! I MUST CONSIDER HOW BEST TO RESPOND TO THE ESCAPIST'S SNEAK ATTACK UPON MY REGIME.
AT ONCE, GREAT LEADER. PERMIT ME TO DISPOSE OF THE OFFENSIVE MATERIAL.
SAFE AND STRONG IS QUODESIA! FOR THIS, WE THANK OUR GREAT LEADER!
SEE YOU AT THE RALLY TONIGHT, COMRADE?
OH... UH, YES. SEE YOU.
ESCAPIST

WEEKS LATER, BENEATH EMPIRE CITY, THE ESCAPIST IS HONING HIS CRAFT.
WHRRRR!
WHZZZZZZ
HOW ARE YOU FIXED FOR BLADES?
HAH! THAT OLD SAW?
"HAH" YOURSELF!
GOOD TO SEE YOU AGAIN, AGENT WALTERS.

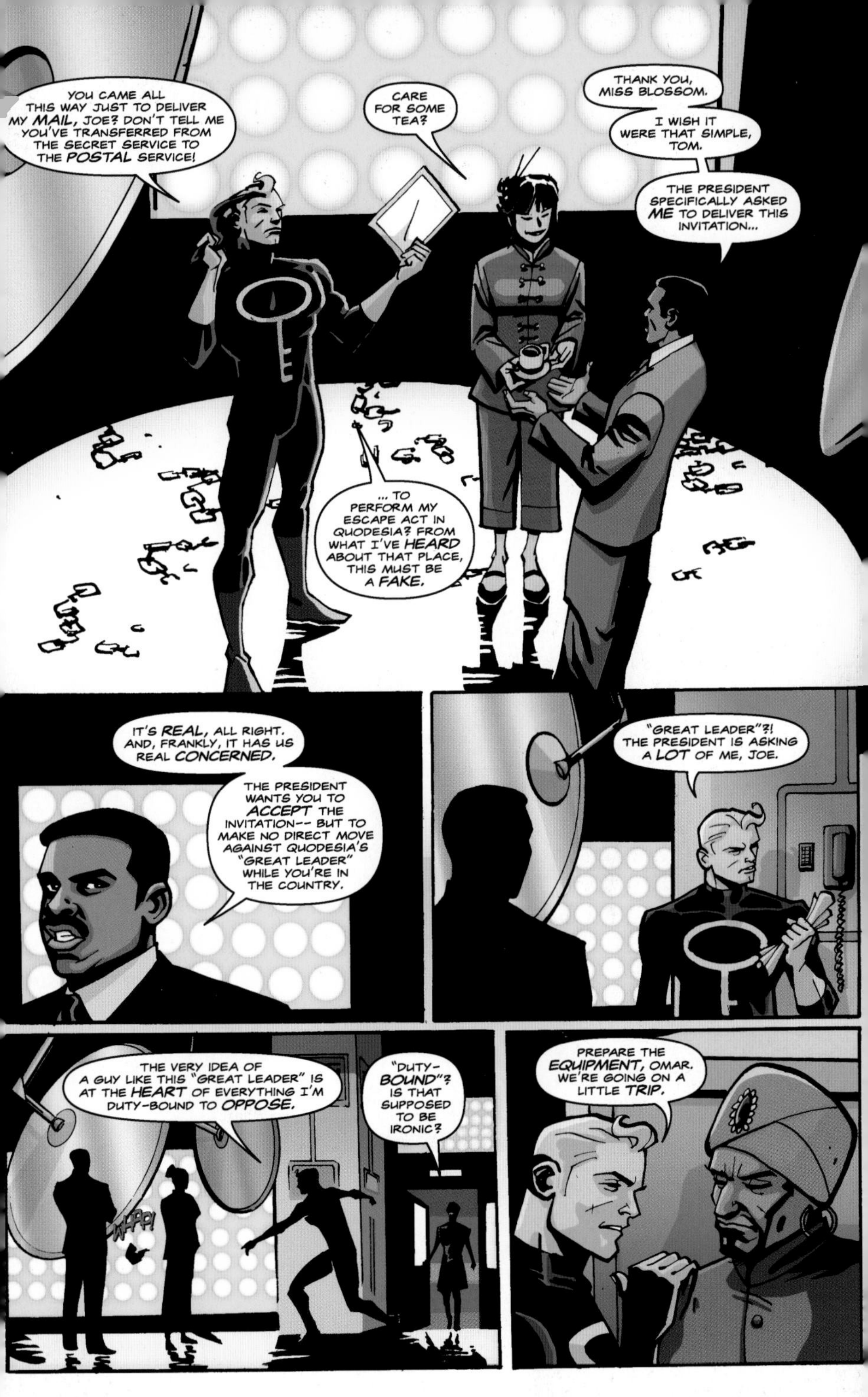
YOU CAME ALL THIS WAY JUST TO DELIVER MY MAIL, JOE? DON'T TELL ME YOU'VE TRANSFERRED FROM THE SECRET SERVICE TO THE POSTAL SERVICE!
CARE FOR SOME TEA?
THANK YOU, MISS BLOSSOM.
I WISH IT WERE THAT SIMPLE, TOM.
THE PRESIDENT SPECIFICALLY ASKED ME TO DELIVER THIS INVITATION...
... TO PERFORM MY ESCAPE ACT IN QUODESIA? FROM WHAT I'VE HEARD ABOUT THAT PLACE, THIS MUST BE A FAKE.
IT'S REAL, ALL RIGHT. AND, FRANKLY, IT HAS US REAL CONCERNED.
THE PRESIDENT WANTS YOU TO ACCEPT THE INVITATION-- BUT TO MAKE NO DIRECT MOVE AGAINST QUODESIA'S "GREAT LEADER" WHILE YOU'RE IN THE COUNTRY.
"GREAT LEADER"?! THE PRESIDENT IS ASKING A LOT OF ME, JOE.
THE VERY IDEA OF A GUY LIKE THIS "GREAT LEADER" IS AT THE HEART OF EVERYTHING I'M DUTY-BOUND TO OPPOSE.
WHPP!
"DUTY-BOUND"? IS THAT SUPPOSED TO BE IRONIC?
PREPARE THE EQUIPMENT, OMAR. WE'RE GOING ON A LITTLE TRIP.

LONG HOURS LATER...
NO WELCOMING COMMITTEE? WE'RE GOING TO NEED HELP MOVING ALL OF THE PROPS FOR THE ACT.
YOU NEED NOT CONCERN YOURSELF. YOUR EQUIPMENT WILL BE CONFISCATED-- BY ORDER OF THE GREAT LEADER HIMSELF.
!
AND NOW, THIS WAY. OUR GREAT LEADER AWAITS YOU.
YOU CHAPS DO REALIZE IT WILL BE DEUCED DIFFICULT TO PUT ON THE SHOW WITHOUT EQUIPMENT?
IT'S OKAY, ALOIS. WE'LL WORK AROUND IT. AFTER ALL, THAT'S WHAT WE DO BEST, ISN'T IT?

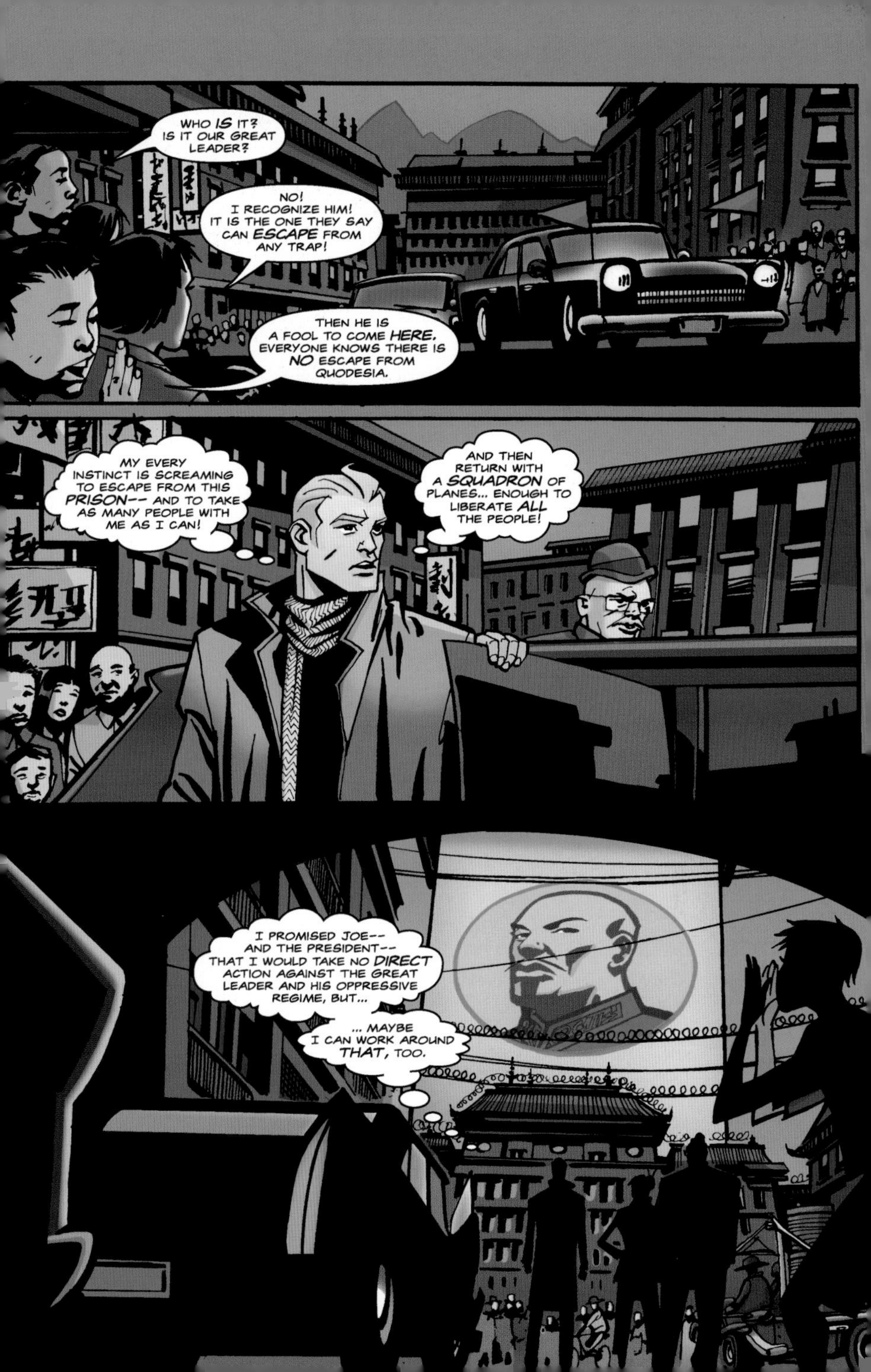
WHO IS IT? IS IT OUR GREAT LEADER?
NO! I RECOGNIZE HIM! IT IS THE ONE THEY SAY CAN ESCAPE FROM ANY TRAP!
THEN HE IS A FOOL TO COME HERE. EVERYONE KNOWS THERE IS NO ESCAPE FROM QUODESIA.
MY EVERY INSTINCT IS SCREAMING TO ESCAPE FROM THIS PRISON-- AND TO TAKE AS MANY PEOPLE WITH ME AS I CAN!
AND THEN RETURN WITH A SQUADRON OF PLANES... ENOUGH TO LIBERATE ALL THE PEOPLE!
I PROMISED JOE-- AND THE PRESIDENT-- THAT I WOULD TAKE NO DIRECT ACTION AGAINST THE GREAT LEADER AND HIS OPPRESSIVE REGIME, BUT...
... MAYBE I CAN WORK AROUND THAT, TOO.

WELCOME, HONORABLE GUESTS! YOU GRACE A HUMBLE NATION WITH YOUR VISIT!
AH, THE ESCAPIST! LONG HAVE I ADMIRED YOUR CAREER. PLEASE, INDULGE A FOOLISH OLD MAN... THIS IS A HISTORIC MOMENT.
COME, COME! YOU ARE THE FIRST TOURISTS EVER TO TRAVEL TO QUODESIA.
THOUGH MY PEOPLE AFFECTIONATELY CALL ME "GREAT LEADER," I AM RATHER MORE LIKE A FATHER TO THEM.
A PROUD FATHER! EAGER TO BRAG... TO SHOW OFF MY-- UH, THEIR-- ACCOMPLISHMENTS.
OF COURSE, AS WITH ANY BIG CITY, THERE ARE DANGERS. AS A PRECAUTION, YOUNG OFFICER YAO-SHI WILL SERVE AS YOUR PERSONAL ATTACHÉ AND BODY-GUARD FOR THE DURATION OF YOUR STAY.
I AM HONORED, SIR.
AS AM I.

"YAO-SHI"? THAT'S THE MANDARIN WORD FOR "KEY," ISN'T IT?
VERY GOOD! I SUPPOSE YOU'D KNOW, BECAUSE KEYS ARE SUCH AN INTEGRAL PART OF THE WORK THAT YOU DO.
HAVING A KEY DOES COME IN HANDY WHEN YOU WANT TO OPEN A LOCK, THOUGH SOMETIMES YOU DO HAVE TO IMPROVISE...
WHICH REMINDS ME... ALL MY EQUIPMENT HAS BEEN CONFISCATED. FOLLOW ME, AND I'LL DRAW UP A LIST OF THINGS I NEED FOR MY PERFORMANCE.
A LITTLE STUFFY IN HERE, WOULDN'T YOU SAY, PLUM?
WHY DON'T YOU OPEN A WINDOW, ALOIS?

WE'RE STUCK WITH A BABY-SITTER, SO YOU CAN'T COME IN. ANY LEADS ON THE UNDER-GROUND?
IT MIGHT TAKE ME LONGER TO MAKE CONTACT THAN WE FIRST THOUGHT-- ASSUMING SUCH AN UNDERGROUND EVEN EXISTS.
THEN WHAT ARE YOU HANGING AROUND FOR?!

WE'RE ALL SET. OUR YOUNG FRIEND WILL MAKE ARRANGEMENTS FOR GOVERNMENT-APPROVED CONSTRUCTION OF A STAGE AND PROPS TO BEGIN TOMORROW.
WHAT DID OMAR HAVE TO SAY?
NO LUCK YET. BUT HOW CAN YOU BE SO CERTAIN QUODESIA EVEN HAS AN ORGANIZED RESISTANCE?

YOU'VE SEEN THIS PLACE, AL... HOW CAN IT NOT?

NEXT MORNING, THE ESCAPIST OVERSEES THE BUILDING OF A HUGE SOUNDSTAGE IN QUOD CITY'S GREAT SQUARE. IT IS HERE THAT HE WILL PULL OFF HIS MOST AMAZING ESCAPE TO DATE.
IF YOU FOLLOW THESE BLUEPRINTS I'VE DRAWN UP, YOU SHOULDN'T ENCOUNTER ANY PROBLEMS. WERE WE ABLE TO GET OUR HANDS ON THOSE SMOKE MACHINES?
NO. PLEASE UNDERSTAND-- MANY SUCH THINGS ARE ILLEGAL HERE.
NOT TO WORRY. I CAN ACHIEVE THE SAME EFFECT WITH SOME DRY ICE.
GO EASY, FELLAS. I'M THE ONLY ONE ALLOWED TO RISK MY LIFE AROUND HERE!
HOW WILL YOU MANAGE TO AVOID BEING IMPALED BY THESE?
IF YOU HAVE TIME, LATER, I'LL SHOW YOU EXACTLY HOW I'M GOING TO DO IT.
?
YOU'RE MAKING QUITE A MESS OF OUR GREAT SQUARE, BUT CONSTRUCTION SEEMS TO BE PROGRESSING SMOOTHLY.
CAN YOU SPARE YOUR BODYGUARD FOR A MOMENT?
I DON'T KNOW. CAN I?
WELL DONE! THE ESCAPIST SEEMS TO HAVE TAKEN YOU INTO HIS CONFIDENCE. NOW YOU MUST LEARN HIS SECRETS AND ARRANGE FOR HIM TO HAVE AN UNFORTUNATE "ACCIDENT."
Y-YES, GREAT LEADER.
DO NOT FORGET WHY WE LET THE ESCAPIST INTO QUODESIA IN THE FIRST PLACE!
201

I HAVE INSTRUCTED THESE MEN TO MAKE A FEW "IMPROVEMENTS" TO THE DESIGN OF THE ESCAPIST'S CONTRAPTIONS.
YOUR JOB IS TO KEEP THE COSTUMED FOOL FROM DISCOVERING THESE CHANGES UNTIL IT IS TOO LATE.
DO THIS FOR ME...
... AND I MAY OVERLOOK THE COLLECTION OF CONTRABAND THAT WAS DISCOVERED IN YOUR ROOM.
HEY, BODYGUARD!
I HAVE NO CHOICE! I MUST DO AS THE GREAT LEADER COMMANDS AND HELP BRING ABOUT THE ESCAPIST'S DEATH!
HOW WOULD YOU LIKE TO STAND IN FOR ME SO WE CAN TEST THIS NEXT STUNT?
REALLY?! I WOULD LIKE THAT VERY MUCH!
TOM, THE BOY HASN'T A HOPE IN THE WORLD OF GETTING OUT OF THERE ON HIS OWN.
THERE'S ALWAYS HOPE, AL. THESE PEOPLE JUST NEED TO BE REMINDED OF THAT.
CLINK!

ELSEWHERE IN QUOD CITY.
DRIVER, STOP THIS CAR AT ONCE!
SHRRRIPP!
UNGRATEFUL PEONS!
YOU! UP THERE! I AM YOUR GREAT LEADER-- AND YOU WILL PAY YOUR RESPECTS, ONE WAY OR ANOTHER!

TOMORROW I'LL TEACH YOU ANOTHER--
I AM TO INFORM YOU THAT THERE WILL BE A BANQUET IN YOUR HONOR TOMORROW.
DON'T LET ME INTERRUPT YOUR GAME, GENTLEMEN. I'M JUST GOING TO LET IN A LITTLE AIR.

WELL? ANY NEWS?
NEWS? MAYBE ONE INTERESTING COLUMN-- AS IN FIFTH COLUMN.
I'VE ARRANGED A MEETING FOR LATER TONIGHT.
BE CAREFUL.
YOU, TOO. CHINESE CHECKERS CAN GET ROUGH!

I'D LIKE TO PROPOSE A TOAST.
TO THE ESCAPIST! LONG MAY HE LIVE!
I SAID... LONG MAY HE LIVE!
DEATH TO ALL BARBARIAN INVADERS!
SHOULDN'T YOU BOYS HAVE WAITED UNTIL AFTER DINNER TO CLEAR THE TABLE?!
BRAKKABRAKKABRAKKA
I AM... PLEASED YOU WERE NOT KILLED.
THIS WILL NOT HAPPEN AGAIN.

LATER, DESPITE THE GREAT LEADER'S COMFORTING WORDS...
THUNK!
EVEN LATER...
OUCH! HEY!
NAJA OPHIOPHAGUS TERRIBILIS. EXTREMELY VENOMOUS. VERY DEADLY.
BELIEVED TO HAVE BEEN EXTINCT FOR DECADES-- UNTIL TODAY, THAT IS.
LUCKY FOR ME, I ONCE MET A MAN IN DELHI WHO SPECIALIZES IN RARE ANTI-VENOM. HE'LL BE HAPPY TO HEAR THAT THE SNAKE AND I ARE BOTH STILL ALIVE.
HE IS IN CONSTANT DANGER HERE IN QUOD CITY, YET STILL HE STAYS TO PERFORM-- AND TO INSPIRE MY PEOPLE.
HE IS A HERO. AND I AM ASHAMED.

REMEMBER WHAT WE TALKED ABOUT BEFORE, YAO-SHI...
YOU AREN'T STRUGGLING WITH YOUR BONDS SO MUCH AS YOU ARE FIGHTING AGAINST YOURSELF.
NNGH!
WHAT ARE YOU UP TO? WHATEVER HAPPENED TO "A MAGICIAN NEVER REVEALS HIS SECRETS"?
THAT'S ONE I WON'T REVEAL, ALOIS!
I'M-- I DID IT! I'M FREE!
KC
CONSTRUCTION OF THE ESCAPIST'S PERFORMING PAVILION IS COMPLETE, AS ARE THE ENHANCEMENTS GREAT LEADER REQUESTED.
SPLENDID. THE EVENT WILL TAKE PLACE AS SCHEDULED, AND I WILL FINALLY BE RID OF THAT "ESCAPE ARTIST" AND THE DANGER HIS PHILOSOPHY REPRESENTS.
OH, AND SEE THAT OFFICER YAO-SHI IS ALSO ELIMINATED. I'M AFRAID CONTACT WITH OUTSIDERS HAS POLLUTED HIM.

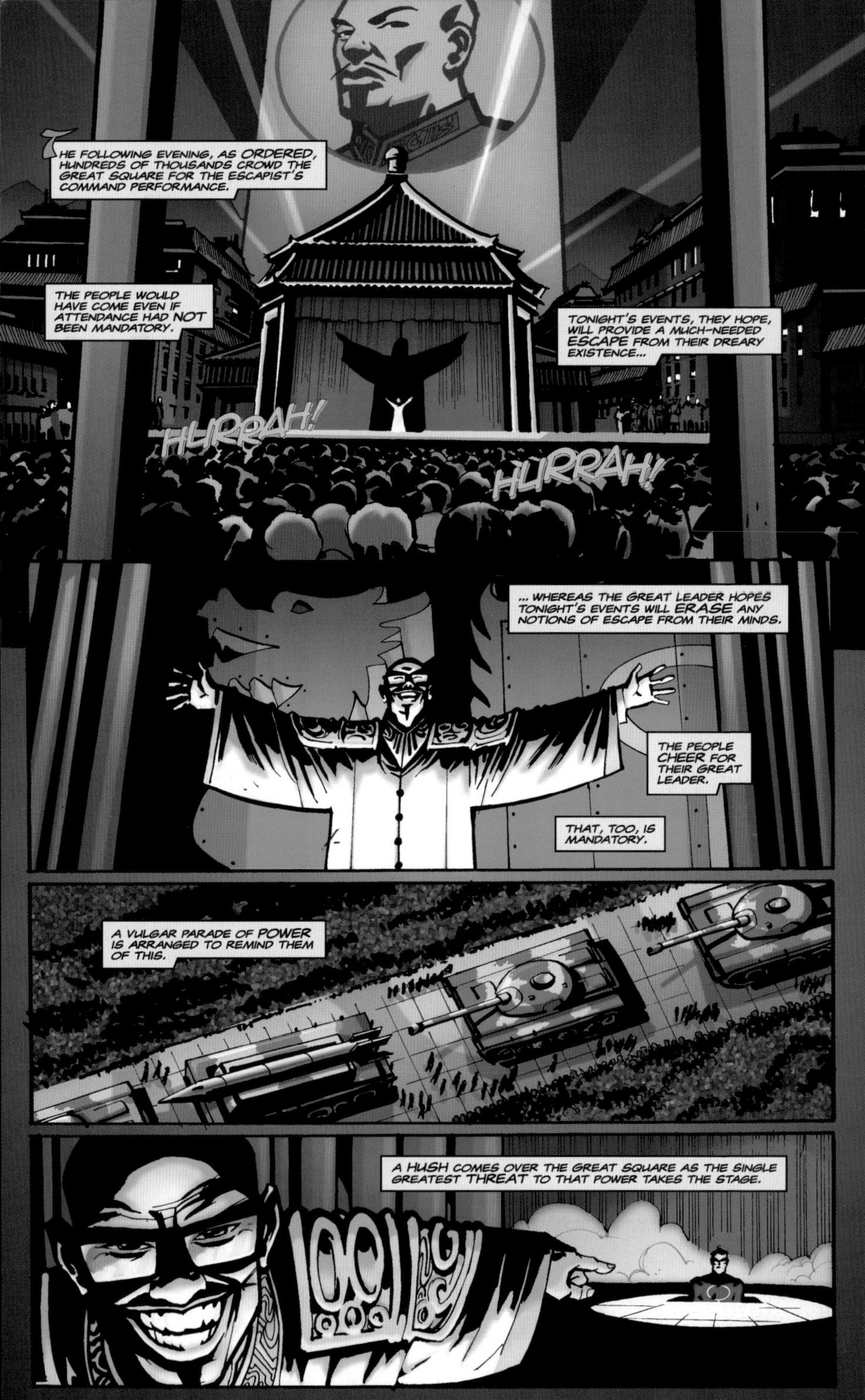
THE FOLLOWING EVENING, AS ORDERED, HUNDREDS OF THOUSANDS CROWD THE GREAT SQUARE FOR THE ESCAPIST'S COMMAND PERFORMANCE.
THE PEOPLE WOULD HAVE COME EVEN IF ATTENDANCE HAD NOT BEEN MANDATORY.
TONIGHT'S EVENTS, THEY HOPE, WILL PROVIDE A MUCH-NEEDED ESCAPE FROM THEIR DREARY EXISTENCE...
HURRAH!
HURRAH!
... WHEREAS THE GREAT LEADER HOPES TONIGHT'S EVENTS WILL ERASE ANY NOTIONS OF ESCAPE FROM THEIR MINDS.
THE PEOPLE CHEER FOR THEIR GREAT LEADER.
THAT, TOO, IS MANDATORY.
A VULGAR PARADE OF POWER IS ARRANGED TO REMIND THEM OF THIS.
A HUSH COMES OVER THE GREAT SQUARE AS THE SINGLE GREATEST THREAT TO THAT POWER TAKES THE STAGE.

AT FIRST, THE CROWD ISN'T SURE HOW TO REACT. THEN, SLOWLY, SOMETHING AWAKENS IN THE HEARTS OF THE PEOPLE.
AND THEY BEGIN TO CHEER AGAIN.
HURRAH!
HURRAH!

HURRAH!
THEY CHEER LOUDER FOR HIM THAN THEY DO FOR ME? WELL, LET THEM.
THOSE CHEERS WILL DIE AS THE ESCAPIST DIES.

BUT THOUGH HE TEMPTS DEATH...

... OVER AND OVER DURING THE COURSE OF HIS PERFORMANCE...

... THE ESCAPIST DOES NOT DIE...

... AND THE CHEERS GROW EVER LOUDER...
HURRAH!

UNTIL THE ESCAPIST'S BIG FINISH.
THE DRAGON MOTIF HAS BEEN CHOSEN DELIBERATELY, AS THE GREAT LEADER IS OFTEN REFERRED TO AS THE "DRAGON OF QUODESIA."
THE SYMBOLISM IS NOT LOST ON THOSE GATHERED IN THE GREAT SQUARE.
AND FOR THE FIRST TIME IN THEIR LIVES, THEY ALLOW THEMSELVES TO ENTERTAIN THE IDEA THAT ESCAPE FROM THE "DRAGON" MAY BE POSSIBLE...
CHUKK!
...AND THAT IS PERHAPS THE MOST AMAZING FEAT OF THE ESCAPIST'S LONG CAREER OF AMAZING FEATS.
HOW... HOW BAD IS IT?
YAO-SHI...
...YOU ONLY HAVE TO ESCAPE FROM THE DRAGON. AND THEN YOU'RE DONE.
YOU WANT ME TO--?!
YOU SAW THEIR FACES.
THE SHOW MUST GO ON.

THE ESCAPIST HAS TO BE THE ONE TO DO IT, BUT ANY ESCAPIST WILL DO. LOOKING THE PART IS EASY ENOUGH.
ALL YOU REALLY NEED IS THE WILL TO BE FREE. THAT'S THE KEY. AND I'VE GIVEN IT TO YOU.
"NOW GO OUT THERE AND REPAY YOUR DEBT OF FREEDOM."
... AN UNFORTUNATE OUTCOME. BUT--
LOOK!
THE ESCAPIST! ALIVE?!
THIS TIME I WILL KILL HIM MYSELF!
WELL DONE, MY BOY. NOW OFF WITH YOU. NO TIME FOR A CURTAIN CALL.
BUT WHERE WILL I GO? THERE'S NO PLACE IN QUODESIA FOR EITHER OFFICER YAO-SHI OR THE ESCAPIST.
THAT MAY BE TRUE NOW, BUT IT WON'T ALWAYS BE SO.
NOW WE HAVE YOU TO LEAD A REBELLION AGAINST OUR NOT-SO-GREAT LEADER.
UH-OH. SPEAK OF THE "DRAGON"!
WHERE IS HE?!

SO... WHAT? IS HE DEAD?
QUITE. TONIGHT WAS THE ESCAPIST'S FINAL PERFORMANCE.
SOB!
MAYBE. OR MAYBE HE'S STILL PERFORMING, EH?
MY CONDOLENCES. THE NATION OF QUODESIA WEEPS WITH YOU.
SATISFIED THAT THE MASTER OF ELUSION IS TRULY DEAD, QUODESIA'S GREAT LEADER ALLOWS THE ESCAPIST'S CREW TO LEAVE THE COUNTRY.
SKREEEEE!

BOOOM!
THE OLD BOY SURE IS THOROUGH-- I'LL GIVE HIM THAT.

I'M AFRAID I MUST ASK YOU TO STOW ALL CARRY-ON LUGGAGE IN THE OVERHEAD BINS.
HOW ABOUT IF I PROMISE TO WEAR MY SEAT BELT INSTEAD?
ALL KIDDING ASIDE, TOM, ARE YOU SURE WE DID THE RIGHT THING BACK THERE?
"I MEAN, WE LEFT THAT YOUNG MAN TO CARRY ON IN YOUR NAME WITHOUT THE BENEFIT OF YOUR GOLDEN KEY."
"OR YOUR SPECIAL EFFECTS WIZARDRY, OLD FRIEND.
"BUT I WOULDN'T WORRY TOO MUCH.
"EVEN AS WE SPEAK, I'M SURE THE NEW ESCAPIST HAS APPROPRIATED OUR EQUIPMENT FOR THE UNDERGROUND.
"I WOULDN'T BE SURPRISED IF ONE DAY SOON HE'S PAID A VISIT BY A MYSTERIOUS STRANGER DRESSED IN WHITE LINEN...
"... AND GIVEN A GOLDEN KEY OF HIS OWN."

"ABSOLUTELY *FAB*-ULOUS!"

A Personal and Idiosyncratic Look at the "Escapist" Comics of the Late 1960s

by Roy Thomas

The following article was scheduled to appear in Roy Thomas's fanzine* Alter Ego*, but got squeezed out by special issues on Julie Schwartz and Jerry Robinson. Roy agreed to let it appear here instead, with the benefit of color reproduction.

"They're 'fab' — and all the rest of the pimply hyperboles!"

With that line of dialogue, a smarmy marketing executive in the 1964 Beatles film *A Hard Day's Night* snidely dismisses his own firm's trendy line of shirts — and, by inference, the Beatles themselves, the "Fab Four" who that year had taken western popular culture by storm.

Those of us who were around during the latter 1960s, however, couldn't afford to be quite so blasé about the Fab *comics* line, which surged briefly onto the scene in late 1965 and blazed like Bill Haley's Comets across the sky before falling to Earth.

It always seemed to me like a four-color monkey wrench tossed into the middle of an otherwise simple situation. Having moved to New York in mid-1965 to work for DC Comics, then jumping ship after two weeks to begin a 15-year stint as Stan Lee's right-hand man at smaller Marvel, I was all geared up to play my part in the David-and-Goliath battle between the upstart Marvel Comics Group and National/DC (the reigning champs ever since 1938) — when, in late '65, a wild card was suddenly tossed onto the table.

I'm talking about … Fab Comics!

Fab Comics was Jerry Glovsky's big chance. Never really one of the big stars in the comic book heavens, even in the glory days of Empire Comics and *The Escapist* back in the early 1940s, he had contented himself with writing and drawing minor heroes like the Snowman. Eventually, with the decline of superhero sales after World War II, he had drawn crime and later horror comics. He'd never quite been able to storm the gates at Lev Gleason's outfit (for one thing, Charlie Biro said he used too many "blacks" in his inking, and Biro's motto was "blacks are cheating"); and his luck was no better at Bill Gaines's EC (though there were rumors he'd once helped Al Williamson, Frank Frazetta, and Roy G. Krenkel on a tight deadline on one particularly exquisite story in *Weird Science*). Eventually he had wangled a staff job in the fabled Marvel (then Timely) bullpen, just in time to be canned along with everybody else during what fans now call the "Implosion" of 1957, when American News went under and sucked companies down with it like a whirlpool.

Now, at fifty, Glovsky suddenly found himself hired as editor by a new company, Fab Comics. Like the other minor players at that time — Tower and Harvey and Charlton and Archie — Fab wanted to take advantage of the sudden surge in publicity garnered by the growing popularity of Marvel Comics and the tide of nostalgia for old comics, as epitomized in the Feb. 15, 1965, *Newsweek* article. (Nobody could have dreamt, just then, that the phenomenal success of the 1966 *Batman* TV show would soon dwarf what had come before.)

The only problem was that, at that point, Fab was nothing but a hopefully attention-getting name and a ravening desire for huge profits. It was left to Glovsky to figure out what to put in the comics.

Looking back to his relationship with Sammy Clay and Joe Kavalier and Empire, it apparently occurred to Glovsky that, in light of what Malachi B. Cohen (in *The Comics Journal*) has called "a gray-lit realm of uncertain ownership," the Escapist and the rest of the old Empire *oeuvre* might well be up for grabs. So he grabbed it.

He sold his bosses on initially publishing a single comic called *The League of the Golden K.E.Y.*, a name which would be trademarkable (which *The Escapist*, at that point, might not be). The "League" part, of course, echoed *Justice League of America*, one of DC's top sellers and the mag that had inspired Marvel's flagship title *Fantastic Four*. "K.E.Y.," which stood for "Keepers of the Enigmas of Yesteryear," was a blatant attempt to latch onto the acronymical craze launched by James Bond's S.P.E.C.T.R.E. and TV's *The Man from U.N.C.L.E.* Hey, if Tower and Marvel could do it, why couldn't Fab?

Glovsky's main problem was talent. Many of his old comic book buddies had long since left the field for commercial art and advertising, and were hardly eager to return to the comic book ghetto. Nor could he expect to lure anyone away from DC, which paid the best rates in the industry. Even those venturesome souls like Gene Colan, Mike Esposito, and Frank Giacoia who yielded to Stan Lee's siren call to moonlight for Marvel did so under pseudonyms, lest they be retaliated against by the turf-protective DC editors.

So Glovsky went after a bunch of newcomers — and struck gold:

Neal Adams, after selling a few pages of gag art to *Archie's Joke Book* and working at Johnstone and Cushing Art Service, had been tapped in 1962 to draw the *Ben Casey* daily comic strip based on the popular TV doctor series; yet somehow he found time to draw a Luna Moth exploit for *League of the Golden K.E.Y.* #1. She had never looked sexier, nor had her curves been rendered more realistically and voluptuously, even though the published strip had to be printed from Neal's pencils and a bit of the delicate linework was thus lost.

Jim Steranko, up from Reading, Pennsylvania, hadn't quite been able to crack Marvel that summer when he journeyed to New York for the first "full-service" comics convention, held at the decrepit Broadway Central Hotel. But he somehow managed to turn his newest sample story — which featured a motorcyle-riding hero reminiscent of scenes in an old Simon & Kirby *Captain America* — into an Escapist escapade. Jim had the added advantage that he wanted to write his own stories.

And Steve Ditko, fresh from his departure from Marvel at the end of '65, would soon be aboard, as well. But not in time for the first issue.

Fab had at least one false start, as well.

During the first half of the 1960s, Gil Kane's star had risen at DC because of his work as the original penciller of editor Julius Schwartz's two popular titles, *Green Lantern* and *The Atom*. By 1965, though, Gil was chafing at the bit to branch out to other companies. He had already pencilled part of a Menthor story for *T.H.U.N.D.E.R. Agents* #1, which hit the stands that autumn, but rumor had it that Fab Comics was paying better page rates than either Tower or Marvel (which wasn't hard — Marvel's rates were roughly half DC's at that stage), so Gil stopped by to talk to his old lunch buddy, Jerry Glovsky.

Glovsky was so eager to get Gil on board that he danced around the subject of rates and persuaded Gil to draw up a few pencil sketches of the Escapist and Luna Moth. Gil even tossed in his own take on Kommandant X (who in the 1950s had switched from Nazi to Commie, and now was about to head the League's acronymical enemy group). As seen for the first time ever on these pages, courtesy of Mrs. Elaine Kane, the artist did fabulous renditions of the characters. For Gil, who felt confined by DC's staid editorial standards, it was a chance to develop the Jack Kirby-influenced side of his style; after all, one of his first jobs had been as assistant/ghost to Simon & Kirby back in the early '40s. Indeed, one of Gil's major complaints about DC was its attitude toward action. As he told me after we began working together in 1969 on Marvel's *Captain Marvel*: "I had to fight Julie [Schwartz] to get him to let me have Green Lantern throw one goddamn punch!"

Gil also admitted that he got a bit annoyed when, without consulting him, Glovsky had a novice named Bucky Gomez ink his sample figures. Not that Gomez hadn't done a stellar job, but another of Gil's motives for going to Fab was that Schwartz wouldn't let him ink his own pencils at DC.

But the real sticking point was money. Fab's publisher had decided he couldn't afford the rates he had originally empowered Glovsky to bruit about, and had retreated to even less than Marvel was currently paying. So Gil stomped out of Fab and strode over to Marvel, where Stan Lee promptly assigned him to pencil an Incredible Hulk story — but over Kirby layouts, and to be inked by Mike Esposito as "Mickey Demeo." Both Gil and Stan were dissatisfied with the resulting art in *Tales to Astonish* #76 (Feb. 1966), and Gil contented himself with drawing for DC, with an occasional foray at Tower, for another year or two.

Glovsky couldn't count on having top established artists come through his door, however, so he put out the word that Fab would be a great place for new talent to make a name for itself.

One early bright spot was Herbert William (Herb) Trimpe. A graduate of the School of Visual Arts, Herb had been inker/assistant to veteran Tom Gill in 1960-'62 and had drawn a spot of Archie in '64, and was eager to get back into the field. His friend John Verpoorten, who was still assisting Gill on *The Owl* and other features for Western, heard about Fab and suggested Herb give it a shot. Herb talked to Jerry Glovsky and was immediately given a rush job, a cover for *League of the Golden K.E.Y. #2*, which showed the hero in battle with the deadly Snapping Turtle, horrific henchman of Kommandant X.

In late 1966/early 1967, Silver Age great Gil Kane pencilled sketches of his own version of the Escapist, Luna Moth, and even a new Kommandant X for the editor of the Fab Comics Group. Inking by Bucky Gomez. *Artwork courtesy of Elaine Kane.*

Herb did several more Escapist stories for Fab until, when Glovsky held back one of his checks during a cash-flow shortage (while Adams, Steranko, and Ditko got paid), the young artist decided that even operating a photostat machine was preferable to working for Fab, so he took that position at Marvel. There, he soon graduated to doing artwork — and later got Verpoorten a staff job, as well.

With Adams, Steranko, Ditko, Trimpe, and others — even without Gil Kane — Fab Comics quickly attracted the attention of Stan Lee, who said to me one day out of the blue, "Why aren't these guys working for *us*?" (He didn't mean Ditko, of course — he'd long since given up trying to understand Steve, or, probably, vice versa.) I had to remind Stan that Steranko, at least, had come up to Marvel looking for work and had been turned down as "not quite ready yet." "Well, next time he comes up," Stan said, "let's grab him."

And, in summer of '66, we did.

A fledgling Herb Trimpe drew this cover for Fab Comics' *The League of the Golden K.E.Y. #2*. *Courtesy of the Rob Lindsay collection.*

WRITING FINIS TO FAB

As Stan Lee's associate editor and the scripter of such Marvel titles as *X-Men* and *Avengers* in the late 1960s, I naturally kept tabs on the competition — and not just DC, either. Besides, I was still fairly fresh from being a wide-eyed, fanzine-publishing comics fan myself, and I bought most anything superhero-oriented that came out.

The two companies (besides DC) that Stan felt most likely to give Marvel a run for readers' coins were Tower Comics, spearheaded by artist/editor Wally Wood, and Fab Comics under Jerry Glovsky.

Tower was probably doomed from the outset, when *T.H.U.N.D.E.R. Agents* and its companion titles debuted at 48 pages for 25¢, while Marvel, DC, et al. were still at 12¢ for 32 pages. I daydreamed of Marvel also reverting to the thicker comics of my youth, but our publisher Martin Goodman figured young readers would rather buy two 12¢ comics than one 25-center … and he was right, dammit. So Marvel and DC thrived, while Tower soon tanked.

Fab avoided that error, but had its own problems. As its rates stayed low, its top talent started to go AWOL. Jim Steranko wandered into Marvel's outer office at the time of 1966's New York comics convention — I showed his sample pages to production manager Sol Brodsky, who in turn showed them to Stan — Jim walked out with the assignment to draw the "S.H.I.E.L.D." strip in *Strange Tales* — and that was the end of his dalliance with Fab Comics. Over at DC, Neal Adams inherited *The Spectre* from Murphy Anderson, which left *him* no time for Fab. And Steve Ditko relinquished his Fab work after he began drawing *The Creeper* and *The Hawk and the Dove* for Carmine Infantino at DC.

Even as Fab faltered, however, the Escapist almost made it into Marvel Comics — at least in a manner of speaking.

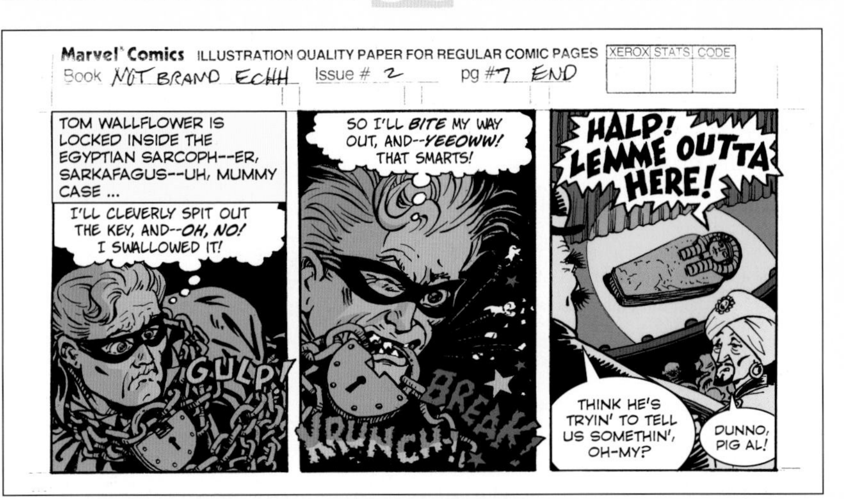

Panels from the Roy Thomas/Marie Severin "Escape-Fist" parody drawn for Marvel's *Not Brand Echh* #2 but never published.

Marvel's new title *Not Brand Echh* lampooned both other companies' heroes and our own. In issue #2 (Sept. 1967), Stan and artist Marie Severin had "Spidey-Man" meet "Gnatman and Rotten," while Gary Friedrich and Marie satirized *T.H.U.N.D.E.R. Agents* as "B.L.U.N.D.E.R. Agents" combating "Knock Furious, Agent of S.H.E.E.S.H." What nobody knows is that "Mirthful Marie" — who from start to finish was the best thing about *NBE* — was originally slated to draw *all three* stories in that issue! What happened was this:

Marie and I had both loved Harvey Kurtzman and Jack Davis's parody of Empire's Golden Age hero as "The Escaper" in the four-color *Mad*, back in 1954. So we did our own takeoff, which I called "The Escape-Fist." Not too inspired — but with "Escaper" already used, what else was left? Mostly, our story poked fun at the Escapist's origin story.

Anyhoo, art and script were virtually completed when publisher Goodman decided we were giving too much publicity to our competitors. Lambasting Batman was fine (Marvel could only gain from parodying him, especially during his TV heyday), and Goodman figured Tower was no threat at its exorbitant 25¢ price. But he nixed an Escapist takeoff. So Don Heck and I hurriedly threw together "Ironed Man" battling "Magnut, Robot Biter" instead. Presumably, Goodman felt Gold Key's *Magnus, Robot Fighter* comic was no real competition.

Through a fluke, Marie and I were never paid for "The Escape-Fist," so art and story belong to us, not to Marvel. Thus, while here we only have room to print a few panels of the story (from photostats that Marvel secretary Fabulous Flo Steinberg held onto over the years*), maybe one of these days *Alter Ego* or some other mag can print all seven pages!

While the above was going on, the *real* Fab Comics was desperately trying to replace the artists (and presumably writers) who'd walked out over low page rates. But the handwriting was on the wall for Fab — and by the end of 1968 the company was gone, crushed like a bothersome gnat between DC and Marvel, who were becoming true rivals now that the latter was no longer distributed by the former.

* And that Ms. Severin colored, all these years later, especially for this publication! —Bubbles LaTour

EVENING THE SCORE

In his seminal *Comics Journal* article "Escapism 101," comics historian Malachi B. Cohen writes that, during the 1960-1968 period, "the battered remnant of Score Comics churned out poorly printed, badly lettered, juvenile (but withal entertaining) crap." How this is different from most other comics of that era he does not elaborate.

"Crap," of course, is in the nose of the beholder. But Cohen is right that some of Score's comics were "entertaining."

The Escapist was such a first-class concept that it inspired writers and artists to come up with good stories, even when the ambitions of their publishers aimed no higher than filling an otherwise vacant spot on the nation's newsstands and, hopefully, luring some unsuspecting breeder of sea monkeys or inventor of X-ray spectacles into purchasing advertising space.

Cohen relates how Score had been formed in 1954 to give DC publisher Harry Donenfeld's nephew-in-law a means of supporting a family. By 1960, name artists like Murphy Anderson, Bob Powell, and others had abandoned the declining Score — Joe Maneely and Jack Cole had unhappily died far too young — and of the various talents Cohen lists as drawing for the company between 1954 and 1959, only Dick Ayers remained, largely because at that stage Stan Lee had little work to offer him besides inking.

While anti-Communist sentiment was more rare in early-1960s comics than in the mid-1950s, there was still a place for it at Score Comics, as drawn by Darlin' Dick Ayers. Courtesy of Dick Ayers.

Ayers's Escapist art of 1960-1963 echoes the excellent work he'd done in the 1950s on Magazine Enterprises' original *Ghost Rider* and *Presto Kid* — which turned out to be good preparation for the Kavalier & Clay hero. The Ghost Rider, after all, had been only a poor underpaid U.S. marshal who tricked owlhoots into thinking he was a genuine spectre — while the Presto Kid, who replaced GR when the newly-formed Comics Code Authority decided ghostly white vigilantes on horseback were too scary for American kids, was just a sleight-of-hand magician in cowboy regalia.

Ayers's art on the early-'60s Score *Escapist* falls midway between *Ghost Rider* and the Jack Kirby-influenced pencilling he'd be doing for Marvel by the turn of 1963. In fact, it was soon after Stan asked him to become Kirby's regular inker on *Fantastic Four* (commencing *FF* #6, Sept. 1962) that Ayers cut his ties with Score. He did so reluctantly, since he generally lived by some good advice given him by a secretary at M.E.: "To keep busy as a freelancer, you should have three accounts." Still, Ayers's gamble paid off, as by 1964 he became the artist of "Human Torch" in *Strange Tales*; in 1965 he likewise inherited *Sgt. Fury and His Howling Commandos* from Kirby.*

* For more details on Dick Ayers's remarkable career, be sure to pick up *The Dick Ayers Story: An Illustrated Autobiography*, published by Mecca Comics Group in graphic novel form, written and drawn by Mr. Ayers himself. —BLT

After Ayers's departure, Martin "Lucky" Lemberg hired virtually anyone who walked in the door to turn out the stories. And they increasingly looked it.

BIG TOP, HI-TONE, OLD HAT

Again quoting Cohen: "Some have argued that [Big Top Comics and Hi-Tone Comics] were in fact the same entity operating under separate names," which "purveyed barely recognizable, in-name-only versions of [the Escapist], intended chiefly to capitalize on all the confusion."

True enough, though by the early '60s there wasn't much left to capitalize on. If Captain Marvel, once the world's best-selling superhero, and Timely's "Big Three" (Captain America, Human Torch, and Sub-Mariner) had no cache during the Eisenhower administration, the Escapist was hardly likely to set hearts dancing during JFK's fleeting Camelot.

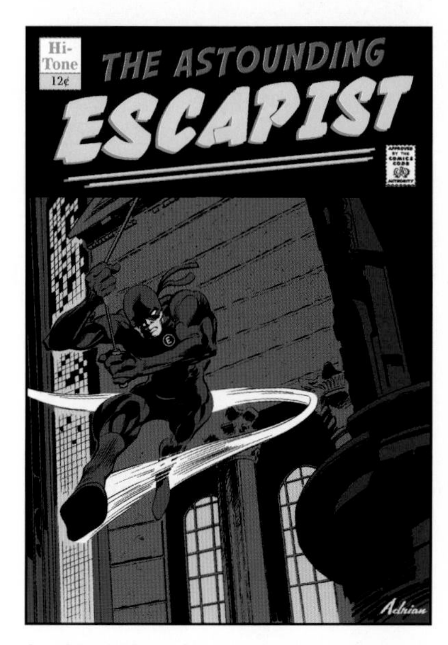

Gene Colan didn't want Stan Lee to know he was moonlighting this cover for the single Hi-Tone *Escapist* comic, so he signed it "Adrian" — a masculine form of the name of his wife Adrienne. *Courtesy of the Glen David Gold collection.*

Big Top's Escapist debuted at roughly the same time (and with the same approach) as Myron Fass and Carl Burgos's *Captain Marvel* — you know, the one who shouted "Split-Zam!" to make his android arms and legs fly off on their own or return to their unsightly sockets. To avoid trademark problems, the Big Top comic was technically titled *The Amazing ESCAPE ARTIST,* although the stories bore "Escapist" mastheads inside ... and this Escapist wore an entirely new costume, with a mask that covered the top half of his head, a cape, and a stylized drawing of a keyhole on his chest. (Presumably the latter was meant to remind readers of the stylized key on the original Escapist's outfit.) Swiping a note from Batman, he also had an Escape-mobile, and entered and exited his secret lair through a so-called Escape Hatch.

Big Top's version vanished after two issues, but three months later a suspiciously similar looking publishing house called Hi-Tone put out a single issue of *The Astounding Escapist,* with a second of what Malachi Cohen calls "barely recognizable, in-name-only versions" of the hero. Hi-Tone's Escapist sported a full-face mask and a circled "E" on his chest. This was perhaps the worst version of all — yet somehow, the editor managed to catch Gene Colan in between Marvel assignments and persuaded him to draw a cover to mask the poorly drawn interiors. It's the only decent part of the entire issue.

IN DYING COLOR

The final entry in the non-existent Escapist Sweepstakes of the 1960s was Conquaire Comics. Again as per Cohen, this was the "publishing arm of Conquaire Grooming Products, manufacturer of hair-care and skin-care products for African-Americans." Cohen turned up the information that Conquaire had somehow become one of Lemberg's "many creditors," and apparently Lemberg stalled for time by giving them the rights to the Escapist.

The most intriguing aspect of Conquaire's 1966 incarnation of the hero, of course, is the fact that he was African-American. Since Score's *Escapist* comic was still limping along, and Fab's entry was called *The League of the Golden K.E.Y.*, while the Big Top/Hi-Tone titles are listed above, Conquaire dubbed its version *The Black Power of the Escapist.* "Black Power" was a phrase just coming into vogue — as was "Black Panther," a name Lee and Kirby used in that year's *Fantastic Four* #52 just as the recently founded African-American organization of that name began to gain notoriety and cause considerable consternation up at Marvel. (Remember T'Challa's brief rechristening as "Black Leopard"?)

While other creative personnel of the Conquaire *Escapist* have yet to be identified, the artist signed his work "Howard Simpson." Whether he is related to the artist who drew various DC and other comics in the 1980s is simply not known.

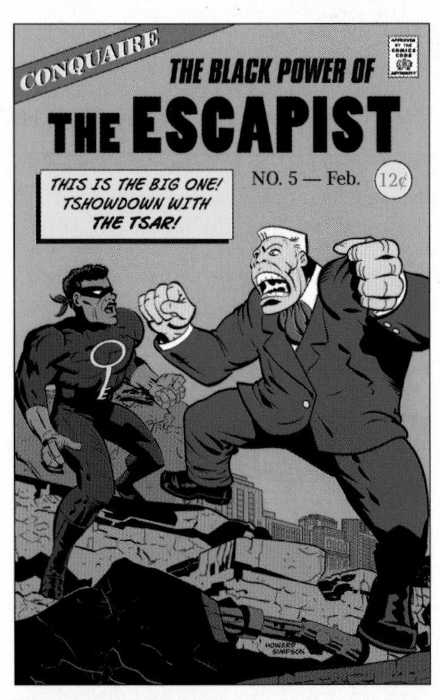

The Conquaire Escapist's grudge match with the "tsinister" Tsar, from *The Black Power of the Escapist* #5 (Feb. 1967) — the final issue. Art by Howard Simpson.

With its black hero/white villains scenario, the comic book foreshadowed such "blaxploitation" films as *Shaft, Superfly,* and *Cleopatra Jones,* which would enjoy a brief heyday a couple of years later. The 1966 Conquaire comic, however, was a bit too far ahead of its time. Many white retailers returned the comics to the distributor in unopened bales, and there weren't nearly enough African-American (and courageous or indifferent white) retailers to make up the difference. It has also been rumored that the less reputable creditors of Marvin Lemberg's Score Comics, whose names ended in vowels, made Conquaire's already unhappy distributor an offer he couldn't refuse, to cancel his comics line. Be that as it may, *The Black Power of the Escapist* died after five explosive issues, which today command high prices in the back-issue market.

LET THE SONNENSCHEIN IN

As Cohen points out: "[I]n 1968, the greeting-card and poster publisher Gerald Sunshine, [Marvin] Lemberg's largest single creditor, succeeded in securing copyright to the Escapist and the other old Empire characters," even if he merely canceled all Escapist-related comics immediately and concentrated on trying to market the hero in other media, including television. But that is a subject for another time and issue.

A major player in early comics fandom, Roy Thomas co-created Alter Ego *in 1961, went to work at Marvel Comics in 1965 as Stan Lee's assistant editor, and by 1972 became Marvel's editor-in-chief. He's written comics extensively over the years, for both Marvel and DC, and although in "semi-retirement," he still continues to shepherd each monthly issue of* Alter Ego, *now published by TwoMorrows.*

THE ESCAPIST
LIBERATORS
n the late 1930s, Nazi
ermany mounted an
mbitious museum
xhibition of what
referred to as
Degenerate Art"...
..modern abstract,
xpressionist, and
urrealistic works
hat reflected
itler's view of the
ewish Problem
nd its negative
mpact on art.
o the chagrin of the
hird Reich, this
xhibition became the
ingle most successful
show ever mounted
n Germany.
After the war, some
hirty percent of the
art from the exhibition
had disappeared
without a trace...
...until now.
WRITTEN & ILLUSTRATED
BY HOWARD CHAYKIN

Paris, mid-August, 1944...
...and though the fact that liberation is barely a week away is ostensibly a secret, everyone knows...
...from the Germans, burning every document they can find...
...to the Resistance, which seems to have multiplied exponentially in the last few days...
...to the Collaborators, who are hoping their neighbors will forgive and forget.
<IT'S BEEN A LONG, LONG TIME.>
<SEVEN YEARS.>
<1937.>
BARCELONA.
LAS RAMBLAS.
<THE BOMBARDMENT.>
<GUERNICA GETS ALL THE PRESS...>
<...BUT WE DIED JUST THE SAME.>
CAFE HOTEL

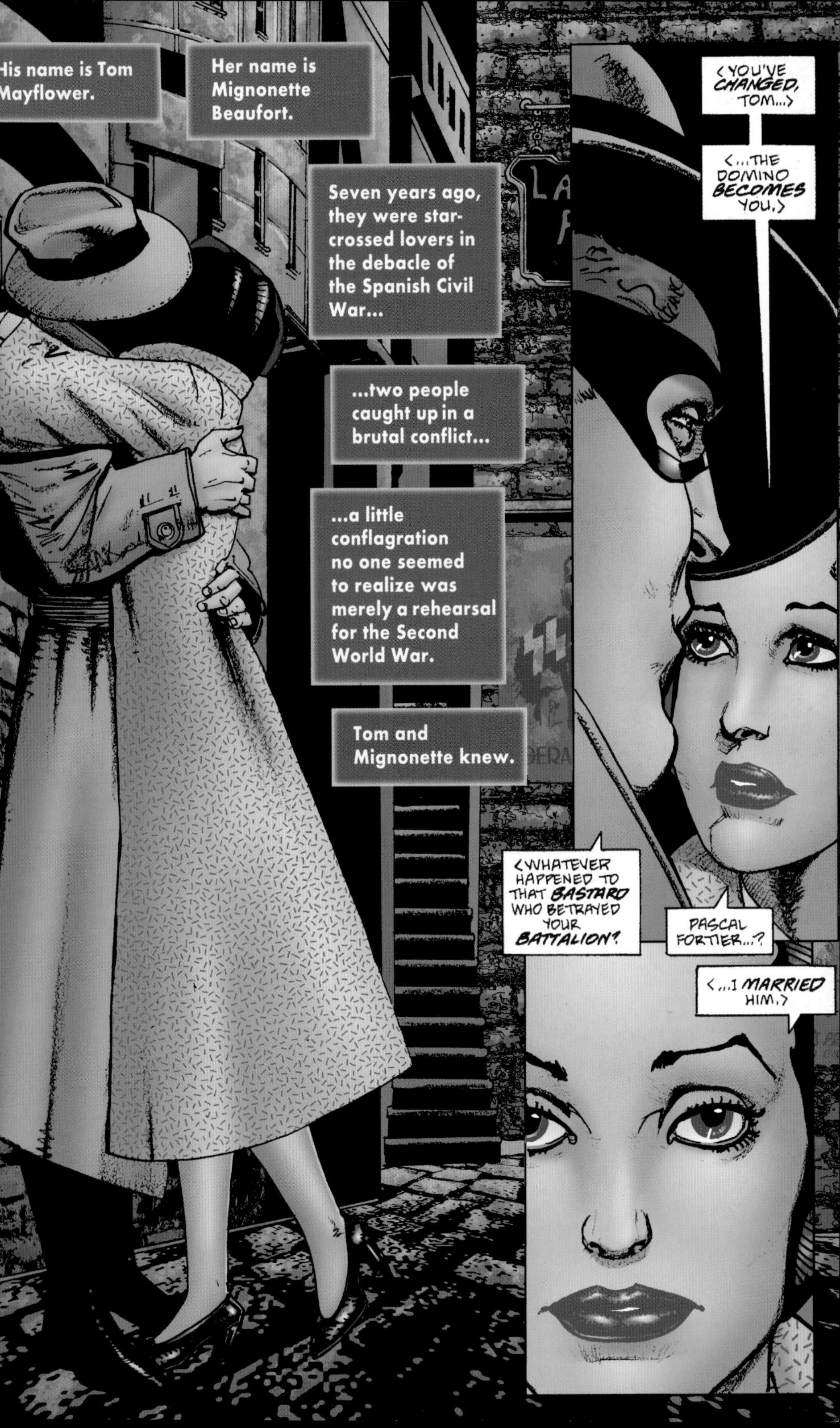
His name is Tom Mayflower.
Her name is Mignonette Beaufort.
Seven years ago, they were star-crossed lovers in the debacle of the Spanish Civil War...
...two people caught up in a brutal conflict...
...a little conflagration no one seemed to realize was merely a rehearsal for the Second World War.
Tom and Mignonette knew.
<YOU'VE CHANGED, TOM...>
<...THE DOMINO BECOMES YOU.>
<WHATEVER HAPPENED TO THAT BASTARD WHO BETRAYED YOUR BATTALION?
PASCAL FORTIER...?
<...I MARRIED HIM.>

<MIGNONETTE TOLD ME YOU'D CHANGED, TOM-->
<--BUT WHO COULD HAVE GUESSED YOU'D TAKE ON YOUR MASTER'S MANTLE?>
<YOU'VE DONE WELL FOR YOURSELF, PASCAL...>
<...COLLABORATION HAS BEEN VERY GOOD TO YOU, IT SEEMS.>
<SUCH AN UNPLEASANT WORD...>
<...I PREFER TO CALL IT PRAGMATIC ACCEPTANCE OF THE REALITY AT HAND.>
<AT LEAST I DON'T RUN AROUND IN A MASK, FOR GOD'S SAKE.>
<NOW--WE CAN SNIPE AT EACH OTHER ALL EVENING...>
<...BUT TIME IS OF THE ESSENCE IF WE'RE TO SUCCEED AT OUR MISSION.>
<MISSION...?>
<OUR UNINVITED GUESTS PLAN TO REMOVE THE MATERIAL TO BERLIN...>
<...TO BE USED AS A BARGAINING CHIP IN THE LIKELY EVENT OF THEIR DEFEAT.>
<LIKELY...?>
<THE GERMANS ARE BLESSED WITH THE ETERNAL OPTIMISM OF THE DELUSIONAL.>
<WILL YOU HELP US KEEP THIS WORK FROM DISAPPEARING FOREVER?>
<ANY HELP I PROVIDE'LL BE FOR MIGNONETTE'S SAKE, PASCAL...>
<...AND WHEN IT COMES TO A PERFORMANCE OF THIS MAGNITUDE, I DON'T WORK ALONE.>

he Department
f Public Works...
...one of the first buildings occupied by the German invaders in June of 1940...
QUAND IL ME PREND DANS SES BRAS...
.its hive of large nd small rooms ırned into a reasure trove f loot.
...and occupied Paris has a plethora of such distractions...
The Escapist's many years on both sides of the footlights have taught him a valuable lesson:
...from the little sparrow, Edith Piaf...
While the udience may elieve the hand quicker than he eye...
...nothing is more effective than slow, deliberate movement...
..aided by a listraction...
...JE VOIS LA VIE EN ROSE.
...IL ME PARLE TOUT BAS...

...to Maurice Chevalier...
AH!—SI VOUS CONNAISSIEZ MA POULE, CA S'EST PASSÉ UN DIMANCHE...
...to Django Reinhardt...
...and, as much as Tom Mayflower would love to sink into the worldly melancholy brought to life by these three great entertainers...
...Tom Mayflower is nowhere in sight...
...while the Escapist has his work cut out for him
German security has always been legendary...
...and the heightened paranoia brought on by the incipient beginning of the foregone end...

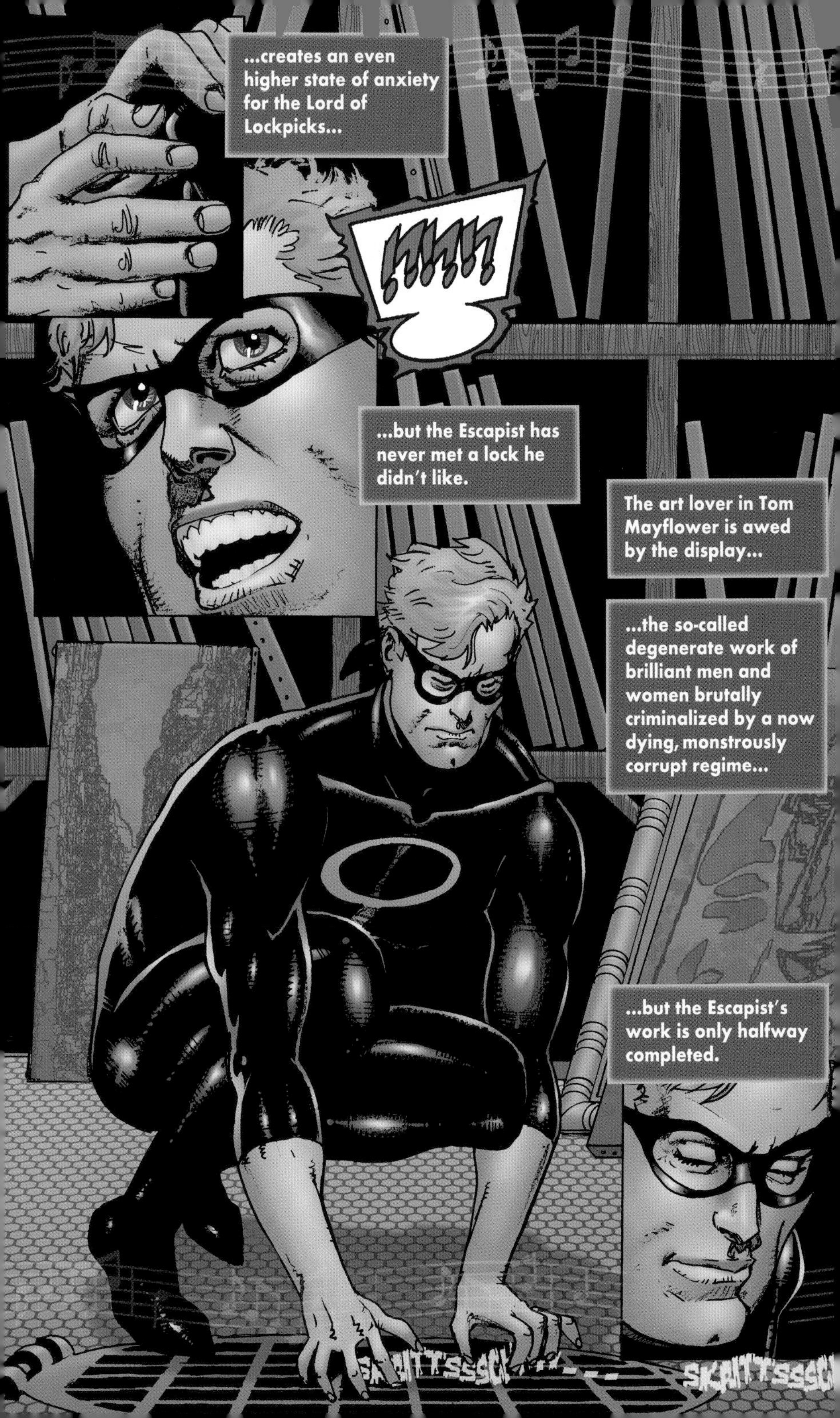

...creates an even higher state of anxiety for the Lord of Lockpicks...
!?!?!?
...but the Escapist has never met a lock he didn't like.
The art lover in Tom Mayflower is awed by the display...
...the so-called degenerate work of brilliant men and women brutally criminalized by a now dying, monstrously corrupt regime...
...but the Escapist's work is only halfway completed.
SKRITTSSSCH...
SKRITTSSSCH

Show business is filled with card handlers, table magicians, and close-up sleight-of-hand artists...
...solo performers with an intimate relationshi p with the audience...
...but it's the rare stage magician or escape artist who works alone...
SKRITTSCCHH...
<IT'S AN INCREDIBLE COLLECTION, MIN...>
<SEVEN YEARS AGO, DESPITE YOUR LIMP, WE DID WHAT WE COULD TO KEEP SOME SMALL TREASURE OUT OF FASCIST HANDS...>
...and the Escapist is no exception...
...but even he never guessed these assistants would come directly from a soundstage...
...where Marcel Carnes works surreptitiously on a film that would come to be known as "Les Enfants du Paradis"...
...a masterpiece of resistance created under the very noses of the occupying army.
<...THE DIFFERENCE TODAY IS THIS TIME WE'VE ACHIEVED MORE THAN A MERE MORAL VICTORY.>

<WHAT NOW?>
<WE BRING THE WORKS TO THE TRAIN, AND-->
<NO, MIN...>
<...I MEAN FOR YOU.>
<PASCAL-->
<PASCAL HAS WHAT HE WANTS...>
<...WHAT IS IT YOU WANT, MIGNONETTE?>
<HAPPINESS...>
CHUFF
<...AND, AFTER ALL THESE YEARS, A LITTLE PEACE.>
<WHAT'S THIS...?>
<... A BIT OF CONSPIRACY AMONG OLD FRIENDS?>
<HARDLY, PASCAL.>
<I WOULDN'T BE SURPRISED, YOU KNOW...>

<...SINCE MY WIFE AND I HAVE HAD OUR LITTLE DIFFERENCES BEFORE...>
<...BUT IN THIS CASE WE ARE A CONSPIRACY OF TWO.>
<MIGNONETTE...>
<FORGET HER, HERO...>
<...IT'S ME YOU SHOULD WORRY ABOUT.>
<I KNEW I COULD COUNT ON YOU TO FALL FOR HER DEWY-EYED LOOK...>
<...WHAT BETTER WAY TO INSURE THESE BOCHE PHILISTINES WOULDN'T GET AWAY WITH THESE MASTERPIECES...>
<...AND THAT YOU WOULD.>

<PRECISELY.>
AU REVOIR...
AU REVOIR, PASCAL...
<...YOU ALWAYS WERE A COMPLETE AND UTTER SWINE.>

<THANKS, MIGNONETTE...>
<...ONE MORE TIME, I OWE YOU MY LIFE.>
<IF ONLY THINGS WERE THAT SIMPLE.>
UNNGGH...!
<PASCAL WANTED THE ART FOR HIMSELF...>
<...YOU WANTED THE ART FOR THE WORLD...>
<...AND I WANT THE ART FOR THE REVOLUTION.>
<IF, BY SOME CHANCE, YOU SHOULD SURVIVE...>

Minutes later...
Urrmm...
...MIGNONETTE...?
"<...THERE'LL BE A LETTER WAITING FOR YOU IN EMPIRE CITY.>"
!?!?!
"<DEAREST TOM...>
"<...IF YOU'RE READING THIS, YOU'VE MADE IT BACK HOME...>

"<...AND I'VE MADE IT BACK HOME, TOO...>
"<...TO MOSCOW...>
"<...AND THE GLORIOUSLY TRIUMPHANT WORKER'S PARADISE...>
"<...THE SOVIET UNION.>
"<WHILE, AS TOM MAYFLOWER, YOU SERVED THE CAUSE OF DEMOCRACY IN SPAIN...>
"<...AND PASCAL SERVED ONLY HIMSELF...>
"<...I COVERTLY SERVED THE GREATER GLORY OF THE WORKERS' REVOLUTION...>
"<...AS A MAJOR IN THE SOVIET POLITICAL POLICE.>

...THE ART WILL FIND A PERFECT HOME IN THE HERMITAGE...>
"<...WHERE IT, TOO, WILL SERVE THE GREATER GLORY OF THE REVOLUTION.>"
WELCOME BACK YOUNG MASTER...
...WE WERE ALL WORRIED ABOUT YOU...
GOOD TO BE HOME, OMAR.
...PARTICULARLY AFTER RECEIVING THAT MOST CURIOUS LETTER...
...I DO HOPE IT WAS APPROPRIATE TO OPEN IT AND CABLE YOU ITS CONTENTS.
ABSOLUTELY, OMAR...
...IT MADE THE CROSSING A BIT EASIER TO TAKE...
...AND IT TOOK SOME OF THE BITE OUT OF MIGNONETTE'S BETRAYAL.
IT SEEMED THAT YOU WERE LESS A VICTIM OF BETRAYAL THAN OF SERVING AS A CONVENIENCE FOR THIS WOMAN.
MAYBE SO...
...BUT I DO OWE MIGNONETTE ONE THING...
...WHATEVER ROMANTIC NAIVETÉ I MIGHT HAVE BEEN CARRYING AROUND HAS BEEN THOROUGHLY BEATEN OUT OF ME.

THE
IN
"LOOK INTO THE ABYSS"
YOU HAVE **GOT** TO BE KIDDING ME...

WHAT? IT'S THE GRAND CANYON! IT'S NATURE! IT'S BEAUTIFUL! AT LEAST GIVE IT A CHANCE.

A CHANCE TO **WHAT?** GET EVEN MORE WIDE OPEN AND DISGUSTING?
I MEAN, I'M SURE THERE'RE CAVES, BUT THAT'D TAKE HOURS TO GET...
GOD! YOU'RE **IMPOSSIBLE!**

NO, I'M **CONSISTENT.** I THOUGHT THE "GRAND" CANYON WASN'T, AND NOW I'M CONSISTENTLY GOING HOME.

WELL... I GUESS IF YOU WANT TO **FREE** YOURSELF... GO ON...

FREE?! WHAT... WHAT DO YOU MEAN?

YOU'RE TRAPPED BY YOUR VERY DRIVE TO BE LIMITED! AND YOU ONLY ESCAPE THE PULL OF THIS DESIRE BY TRAPPING YOURSELF!

SO IT'S FREEDOM YOU'RE SEEKING! FROM THE GNAWING IMPULSE IN YOUR MIND!

i feel... so... dirty...
ESCAPE! FREEDOM! YOU'RE A TOTAL HYPOCRITE!

HIPPO-THIS!

THAT IS **IT!** I'VE **HAD IT!** YOU'RE... YOU'RE **GROUNDED!**

YOU CAN **DO** THAT?
YES, OKAY? YOU WIN!

THIS TRIP TURNED OUT GREAT! WE SHOULD HAVE DONE THIS YEARS AGO!

The ESCAPIST in "a Fair to Remember"

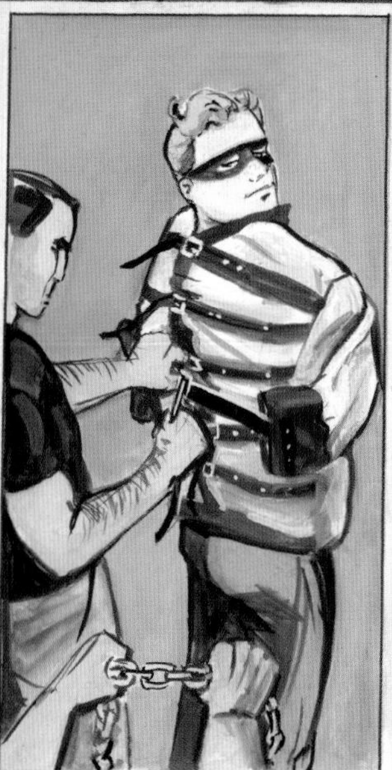

THIS IS A MOST UNEXPECTED TURN OF EVENTS. I HAD NOT INCLUDED THE ESCAPIST IN MY CALCULATIONS.

HE WILL NEED TO BE DEALT WITH IMMEDIATELY IF WE ARE TO PROCEED TONIGHT.

WHY, I MIGHT BE ABLE TO...HOW DO THE AMERICANS SAY...KILL TWO BIRDS WITH ONE STONE?

I CAN RID THE IRON CHAIN OF ITS GREATEST ENEMY...
...AND SIMULTANEOUSLY CRUSH THE MORALE OF THE AMERICAN PEOPLE BY DESTROYING THE VERY ESSENCE OF THIS "WORLD'S FAIR"...
...THEIR BELIEF IN AN AMERICAN FUTURE.

AND REMEMBER... I MAY HAVE ESCAPED THESE CHAINS, BUT NO MAN CAN ESCAPE THE FUTURE!
SO MAKE SURE YOU SEE THE FUTURE TODAY, AT THE UNITED MOTORS FUTURAMA EXHIBIT.
WELL, PLUM, SO FAR, SO GOOD. THE ESCAPE WENT OFF WITHOUT A HITCH. AND NO SIGN OF THE IRON CHAIN.
THAT'S A RELIEF. FOR ONCE WE CAN RELAX. THERE'S SO MUCH TO SEE HERE: THE PERISPHERE, THE TIME CAPSULE...
THEIR LACK OF PRESENCE IS EXACTLY WHAT I'M WORRIED ABOUT. IT INDICATES THAT THE IRON CHAIN'S PLAN MUST BE ALL THE MORE SINISTER.
GOLDEN KEY INTELLIGENCE HAS NEVER FAILED US, OMAR.
IF THEY SAY THE IRON CHAIN IS HERE—
KNOCK KNOCK
A GERMAN BUSINESSMAN WANTS TO SPEAK TO YOU.
A GERMAN! HERE! I'D BETTER KEEP MY WITS ABOUT ME.
AH! THE GREAT ESCAPIST. MY NAME IS SCHNEIDER. I'M THE MANAGER OF THE AMERICAN OPERATIONS OF THE PEOPLE'S MOTORS.

YOUR DISPLAY WITH THE AMERICAN-MADE ROADSTER VAS IMPRESSIVE. MY EMPLOYER VOULD LIKE TO ENGAGE YOU TO REPEAT YOUR PERFORMANCE, BUT VITH OUR NEWEST VEHICLE, THE PEOPLE'S VAGON.
HE'S OBVIOUSLY AN AGENT OF THE IRON CHAIN, TRYING TO LURE ME INTO SOME KIND OF TRAP. I'LL GO ALONG WITH HIM FOR NOW.
WHY, CERTAINLY, HERR SCHNEIDER. THE ESCAPIST IS ALWAYS LOOKING FOR A NEW CHALLENGE.
THAT IS GOOT, FOR VE AT THE PEOPLE'S MOTORS BELIEVE NOT EVEN THE GREAT ESCAPIST CAN ESCAPE FROM THE ULTIMATE AUTOMOBILE.
LEAD THE WAY!
NO EVIDENCE YET OF THE IRON CHAIN'S INVOLVEMENT. MAYBE HIS INVITATION IS GENUINE. I SUPPOSE NOT ALL GERMANS ARE IN LEAGUE WITH THE IRON CHAIN. ...OR ARE THEY?
IT HAS A UNIQUE AERODYNAMIC DESIGN.
AND YET SO STYLISH, ALOIS.
JA! UND IT IS POWERED BY LEADING GERMAN TECHNOLOGY. VOULD YOU LIKE TO SEE?

IT HAS NO ENGINE!
PRECISELY! BUT IT HAS SOMETHING EVEN BETTER.
ghssspp.
-KOFF!-
choke!
THE IRON CHAIN! THE INTELLIGENCE WAS RIGHT.
WHERE IS THE ESCAPIST?
DO NOT VORRY ABOUT YOUR FRIEND. HE HAS JUST TAKEN A SHORT TRIP...
TO THE SEVENTIETH CENTURY!
WHAT DOES HE MEAN? MY GOD! THE EMPIRE CITY TIME CAPSULE...
IT'S BEING BURIED TONIGHT!

LADIES AND GENTLEMEN, OUR LAST EVENT FOR TODAY WILL BE THE BURYING OF THE TIME CAPSULE, OUR MESSAGE TO THE PEOPLE OF THE FUTURE!
CONTAINED IN THIS LARGE ALUMINUM TUBE IS A CROSS-SECTION OF ITEMS REPRESENTING 20TH-CENTURY CULTURE...
THE WORKS OF THOMAS MANN.
COPIES OF *LIFE* MAGAZINE.
A KEWPIE DOLL.
A DOLLAR IN CHANGE.
A PACK OF CIGARETTES.
A ZIPPO LIGHTER.
AND MORE.
THE CAPSULE WILL BE PLACED AT THE BOTTOM OF A FIFTY-FOOT SHAFT AND SEALED IN PLACE, NOT TO BE OPENED UNTIL 6940 A.D.
GENTLEMEN...
LOWER THE CAPSULE.

WHERE IN BLAZES AM I?
TIGHT SPACE...
WAIT!

THE GOLDEN KEY ALWAYS SHEDS LIGHT ON A DARK SITUATION. THIS STRUCTURE LOOKS FAMILIAR.

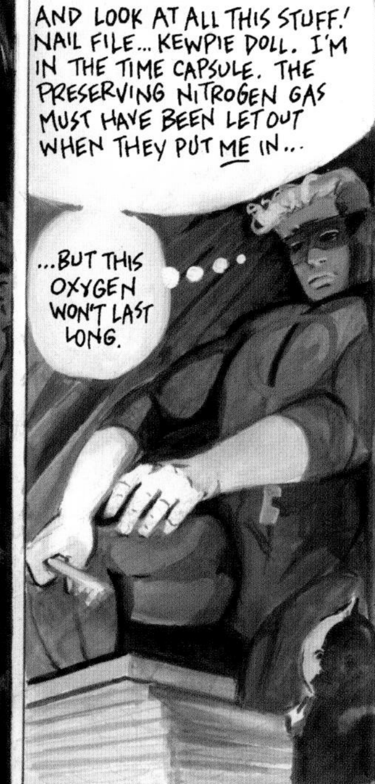
AND LOOK AT ALL THIS STUFF! NAIL FILE... KEWPIE DOLL. I'M IN THE TIME CAPSULE. THE PRESERVING NITROGEN GAS MUST HAVE BEEN LET OUT WHEN THEY PUT ME IN...
...BUT THIS OXYGEN WON'T LAST LONG.

EED TO CLEAR MY MIND. HOMAS MANN SHOULD DO THE RICK. LET'S SEE..."WHEN SPRING, THE FAIREST SEASON OF THE EAR, DOES HONOR TO ITS NAME, ND WHEN THE TRILLING OF THE IRDS ROUSES ME EARLY BECAUSE HAVE ENDED THE DAY BEFORE T A SEEMLY HOUR"...
Hmmm.
THOMAS MANN

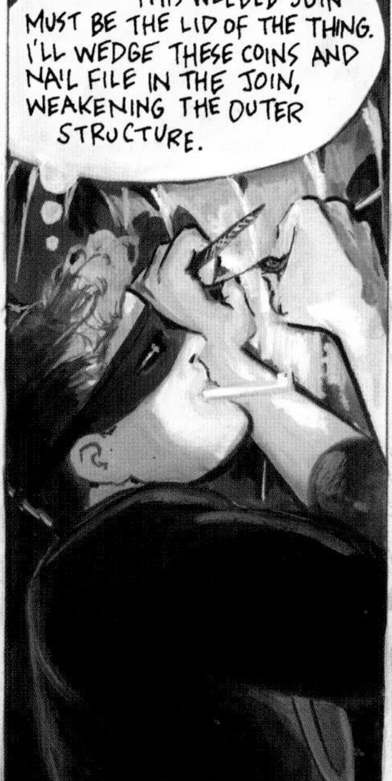
A PLAN. THIS WELDED JOIN MUST BE THE LID OF THE THING. I'LL WEDGE THESE COINS AND NAIL FILE IN THE JOIN, WEAKENING THE OUTER STRUCTURE.

NOW THE CERAMIC KEWPIE DOLL.

OFF WITH HEAD... POUR IN THE LIGHTER FUEL... SEAL WITH THE CHEWING GUM. INSTANT BOMB!

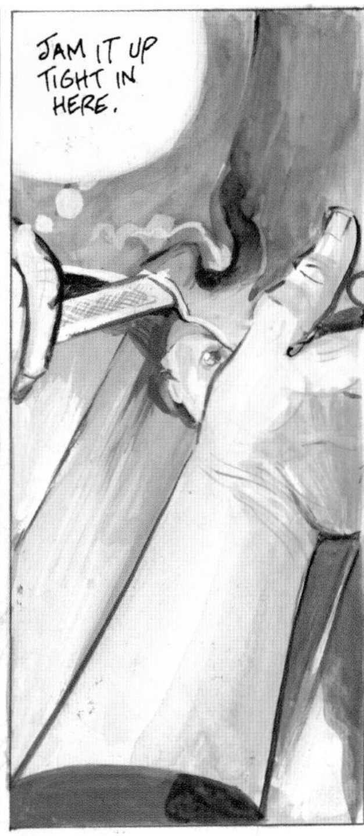
JAM IT UP TIGHT IN HERE.

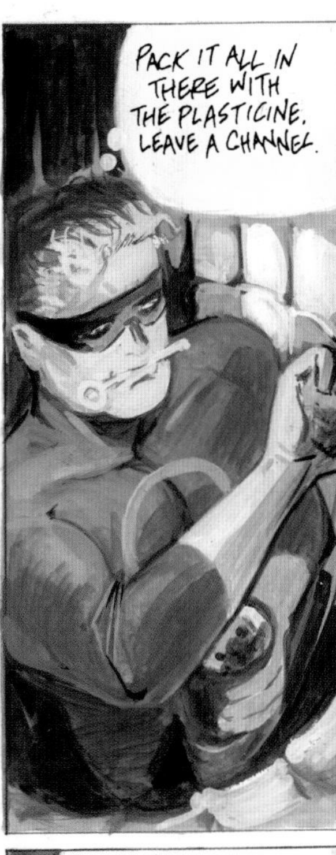
PACK IT ALL IN THERE WITH THE PLASTICINE. LEAVE A CHANNEL.

JUST ENOUGH GAS FOR ONE ATTEMPT...I'M NO SMOKER, BUT TWO PUFFS ...AND I HAVE A SHORT FUSE -
: KOFF :

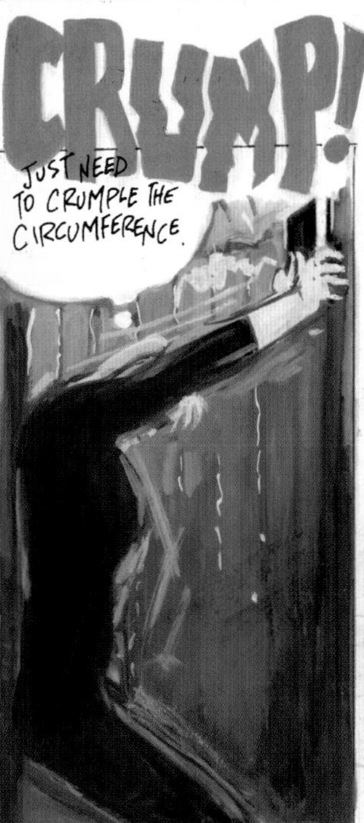
CRUMP!
JUST NEED TO CRUMPLE THE CIRCUMFERENCE.

THEN THE HOOD CAN BE PUSHED OFF... AND THE MANHOLE COVER... WELL, THAT'S JUST "BUSINESS AS USUAL" FOR — THE ESCAPIST!
TIME CAPSULE
OF THE WORLD'S FAI
EMPIRE CITY
1940AD
TO BE OPENED
6940AD

THE SENSATIONAL PARACHUTE DROP. BUT WITHOUT A PARACHUTE, IT BECOMES JUST A DROP - A DROP TO YOUR DEATH, JA?

AH, YOU AMERICANS! ALWAYS YOU THINK YOURS IS THE ONLY VISION OF THE FUTURE. BUT THIS WHOLE EVENT, THIS "VORLD OF TOMORROW," IT IS ALL FALSE. THE FUTURE STANDS BEFORE YOU. VE, THE *IRON CHAIN*, ARE THE FUTURE.

AND VHAT BETTER VAY TO DESTROY HOPE FOR THE FUTURE THAN TO DESTROY THE FUTURAMA EXHIBIT!

BUT VE VILL VAIT UNTIL TOMORROW, WHEN IT IS FULL OF NAIVE AMERICANS.

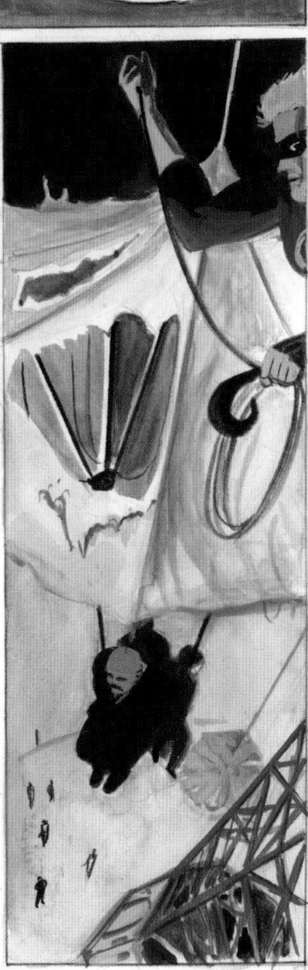

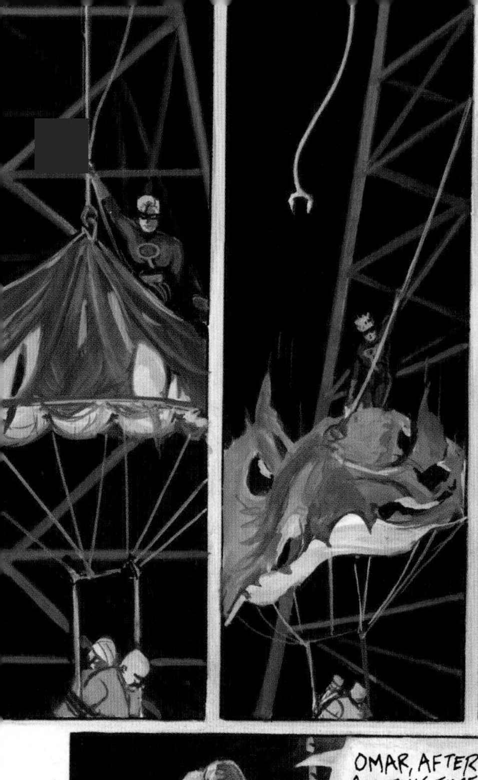
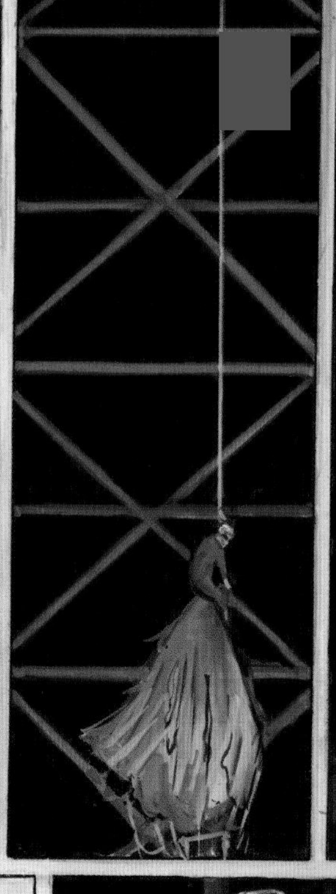
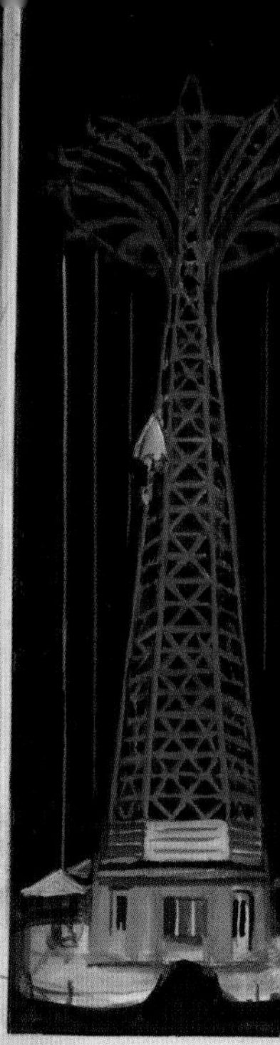

I CAN'T BELIEVE IT'S YOU! I WAS SURE EVEN YOU COULD NOT ESCAPE THE TIME CAPSULE !!
OMAR, AFTER ALL THIS TIME, YOU KNOW THAT MY STRUGGLE AGAINST OPPRESSION WILL NEVER END.

BUT WHAT OF THE IRON CHAIN'S PLAN?
I MADE A PHONE CALL TO THE POLIC SHORTLY AFTER MY ESCAPE. PUT IT THIS WAY...
I SEE NO FUTURE IN THAT PLAN.

ESCAPIST, YOU'VE SAVED THE WORLD'S FAIR FROM CERTAIN DISASTER. AS YOU KNOW, WE HAVE BEEN STRUGGLING FINANCIALLY FOR SOME TIME NOW, AND AN INCIDENT LIKE THIS WOULD HAVE PUSHED US OVER THE EDGE.
WE BOTH KNOW HOW IMPORTANT THIS FAIR IS, MR. CHAIRMAN. WITH ALL THE TROUBLE IN EUROPE, WE NEED HOPE FOR THE FUTURE. KEEP UP THE GOOD WORK.
WE WILL. AND THANKS AGAIN FOR YOUR CONTRIBUTION TO THE NEW CAPSULE.
AND WHAT WAS YOUR CONTRIBUTION, EXACTLY?
OH, JUST MY PERSONAL MESSAGE TO THE PEOPLE OF THE FUTURE.

EMPIRE CITY, 6940.

THE DEPARTMENT OF ANCIENT HISTORY.

ZHUM

A PERSONAL GROOMING DEVICE, PERHAPS?

OGETHER FOR THE FIRST TIME ON ONE STAGE!
THE PHYSICIAN of ILLUSION & THE MASTER of ELUSION
YOU KNOW ME.
I AM ANTON D'GARDO, DOCTOR HYPNOSIS ...
I AM KNOWN AND FEARED THROUGHOUT THE LAND ...
FOR I AM THE MAN WHO DESTROYED THE ESCAPIST!
HYPNOSIS
THE ESCAPIST
ONIGHT - FOR ONE NIGHT ONLY!
BODY & MIND TESTED BE LIMITS!

MIND YOU, THAT'S NOT MUCH OF AN ACHIEVEMENT.
I'VE ALWAYS THOUGHT HE WAS OVER-RATED.
HE JUST MADE EASY ESCAPES LOOK DIFFICULT.
DON'T BELIEVE ME? OKAY, LET'S TAKE A CLOSER LOOK AT THIS "ESCAPE."
HE USES A LOCKPICK HIDDEN IN HIS CHEEK TO OPEN THE CHAINS ROUND HIS HANDS...
WHILST A TRICK RELEASE MEANS THE FOOT CHAINS FALL OPEN AT THE SAME TIME.
THE FIRE BELOW ISN'T ENOUGH TO BOIL AN EGG, LET ALONE A TANK OF WATER...

ALL IT DOES IS SOFTEN THE GLUE HOLDING THE SIDES OF THE GLASS BOX TOGETHER.
ONE SHARP KICK AND THE WATER GUSHES OUT, EXTINGUISHING THE FIRE.
AND IN A SINGLE BOUND OUR HERO IS FREE ...
oh YES.. BRAVO! WELL DONE!
"SHOW-MAN," THAT'S WHAT HE CALLS HIMSELF.
"SHOW-OFF"!
THAT'S WHAT I CALL IT!

WHAT PEOPLE WANT TO SEE IS THE SPECTACLE ...
SOME-THING TRULY ASTONISHING. SOMETHING MARVELOUS.
SOME-THING SO DARING ...SO DAZZLING ...
...THEY WON'T EVEN BELIEVE WHAT THEY REALLY SAW.
THAT'S SOMETHING PEOPLE WILL PAY GOOD MONEY TO SEE!
DID YOU SEE THAT?
ASTONISHING!
I COULDN'T BELIEVE IT ...
MARVELOUS!
...TAKE MY JEWELS ...
DAZZLING!
-- SO DARING ...
WILL YOU TAKE A CHECK?

YOU'VE BEEN A MOST GENEROUS AUDIENCE.

GOOD NIGHT!
POP!

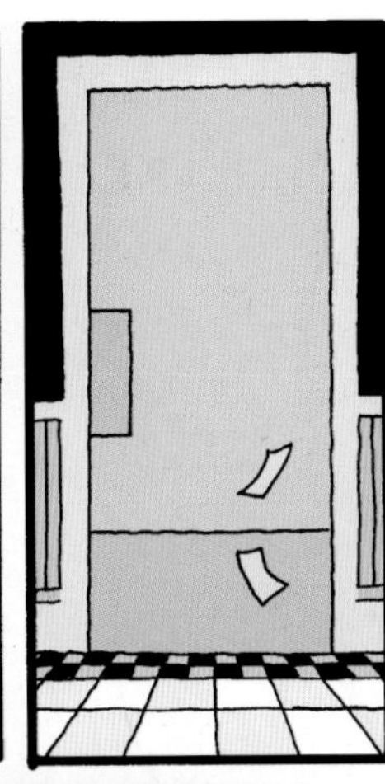

RAH! YAY! CLAP CLAP
"DID YOU SEE THAT?"

HE JUST WALKED THROUGH THE DOOR ...
AND EVERYONE'S ACTING LIKE HE'S VANISHED!
HE'S VERY GOOD ...
HOW DOES HE DO IT?

THAT'S A VERY GOOD QUESTION, PLUM.
AND I THINK I OUGHT TO FIND AN ANSWER!

SOMEONE'S GOT THEIR NOSE PUT OUT OF JOINT...
COME ON, AL ...
WE'D BETTER MAKE SURE HE KEEPS OUT OF TROUBLE.

IT'S NOT THEFT.
I ONLY TAKE WHAT PEOPLE GIVE ME. FREELY.
OF COURSE, THERE WILL ALWAYS BE JEALOUS PEOPLE WHO FAIL TO UNDERST ...
I'VE SEEN YOUR ACT, D'GARDO ...
THOSE PEOPLE DIDN'T GIVE YOU ANYTHING FREELY ...
YOU'VE ALREADY TAKEN THAT FREEDOM!
WELL, THAT KIND OF TRICK DOESN'T WORK ON ME!
PLEASE ...
LET ME EXPLAIN, THEN PERHAPS YOU'LL UNDER-STAND ...
..I..
..I..

I SUPPOSE YOU'VE SEEN EVERY KIND OF ACT IN YOUR DAY.
I DON'T EXPECT YOU TO FALL FOR MINE!
CAN'T MOVE...
BUT THE DIFFERENCE IS, MY FRIEND,
MINE ISN'T AN ACT!
I HAVE THE POWER!
I ONLY SUGGEST THE IDEA AND IT BECOMES TRUE!
FORGIVE THE INTRUSION, DOC, BUT...
TOM!
Ah! TWO OF THE ESCAPIST'S ENTOU-RAGE!
PLUM BLOSSOM AND BIG AL, ISN'T IT?
WELL, I'D LOVE TO STICK AROUND AND SWAP STAGE STORIES WITH YOU ...

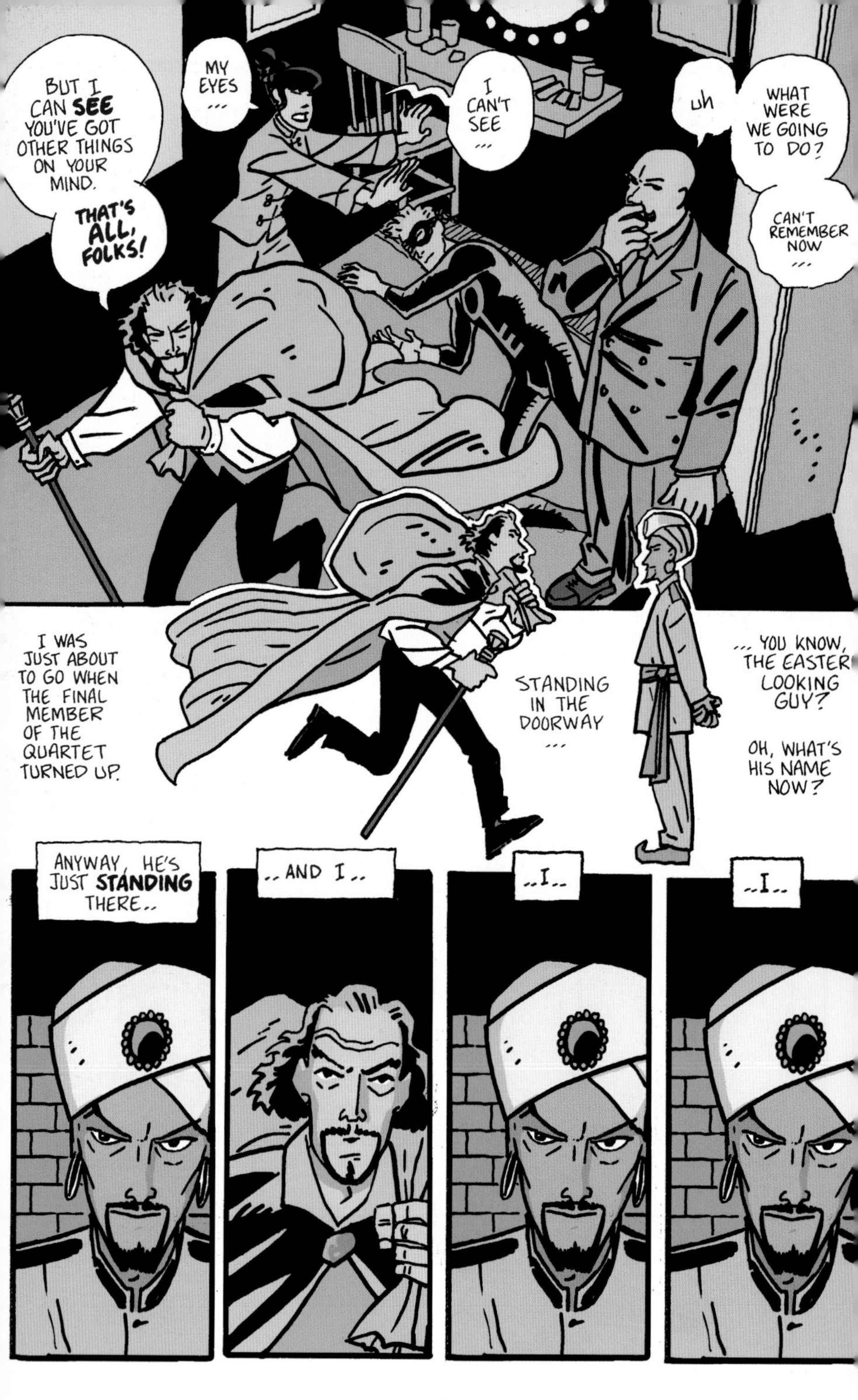
BUT I CAN SEE YOU'VE GOT OTHER THINGS ON YOUR MIND.
THAT'S ALL, FOLKS!
MY EYES ...
I CAN'T SEE ...
uh
WHAT WERE WE GOING TO DO?
CAN'T REMEMBER NOW ...
I WAS JUST ABOUT TO GO WHEN THE FINAL MEMBER OF THE QUARTET TURNED UP.
STANDING IN THE DOORWAY ...
... YOU KNOW, THE EASTER LOOKING GUY?
OH, WHAT'S HIS NAME NOW?
ANYWAY, HE'S JUST STANDING THERE..
.. AND I ..
..I..
..I..

... I WHACKED HIM WITH MY BAG OF LOOT AND MADE MY **ESCAPE!**
THE TIMES
ARISE, SIR ANTON D'GARDO!
QUEEN KNIGHTS DOC HYPNOSIS!
THE GLOBE
DOC HYPNOSIS TO PERFORM FOR THE PRESIDENT!
OF COURSE, THE PAPERS WERE FULL OF THE STORY ...
PEOPLE WERE QUEUING ROUND THE BLOCK TO SEE MY SHOW!
SOON, ALL THE WEALTH AND POWER I EVER WANTED WAS **MINE!**
PRESIDENTS AND PRINCES BOW BEFORE ME! NO ONE WOULD DARE TO CHALLENGE ME!
I AM ANTON D'GARDO, DOCTOR **HYPNOSIS** ...
I AM KNOWN AND **FEARED** THROUGHOUT THE LAND ...

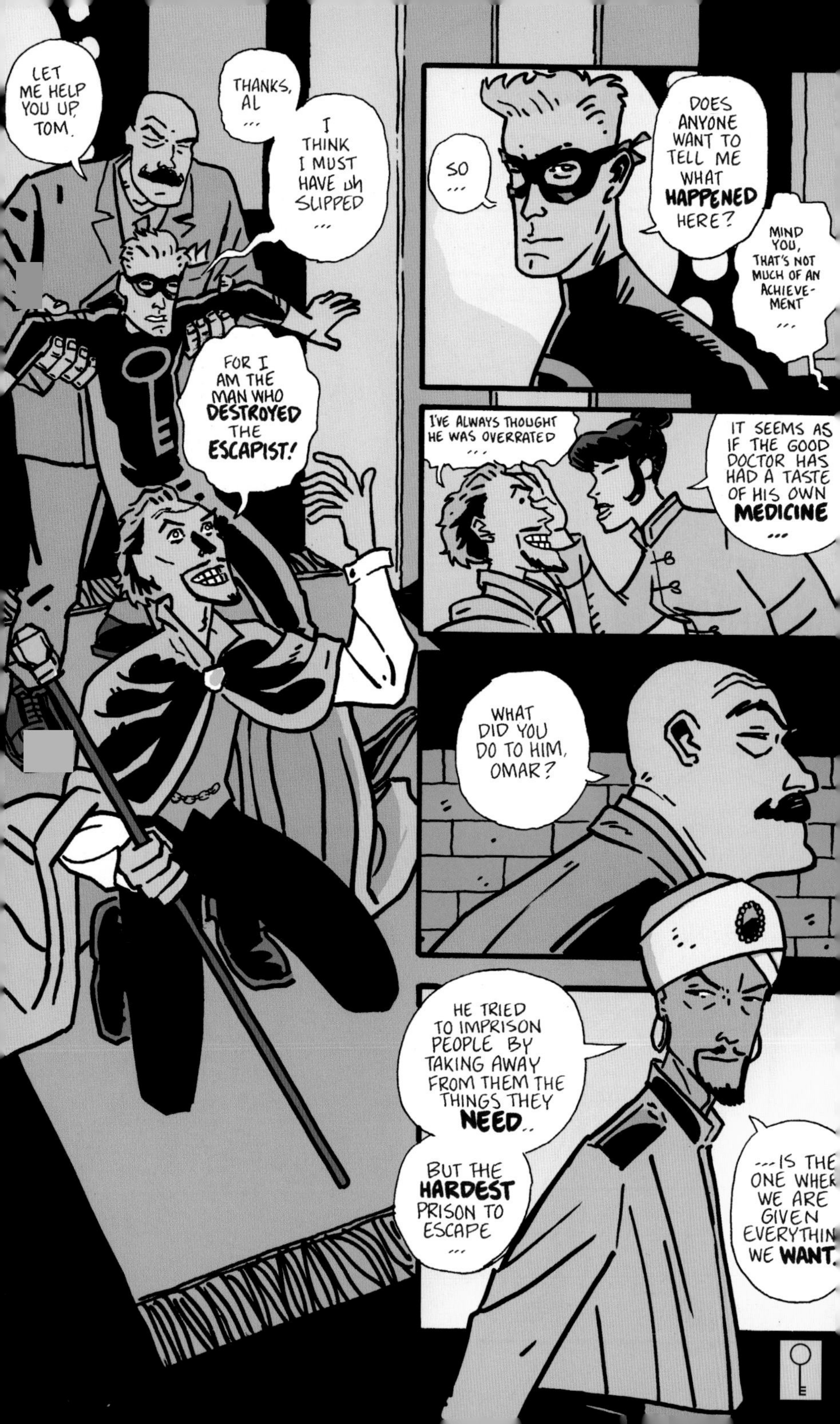
LET ME HELP YOU UP, TOM.
THANKS, AL ...
I THINK I MUST HAVE uh SLIPPED ...
FOR I AM THE MAN WHO DESTROYED THE ESCAPIST!
SO ...
DOES ANYONE WANT TO TELL ME WHAT HAPPENED HERE?
MIND YOU, THAT'S NOT MUCH OF AN ACHIEVE-MENT ...
I'VE ALWAYS THOUGHT HE WAS OVERRATED ...
IT SEEMS AS IF THE GOOD DOCTOR HAS HAD A TASTE OF HIS OWN MEDICINE ...
WHAT DID YOU DO TO HIM, OMAR?
HE TRIED TO IMPRISON PEOPLE BY TAKING AWAY FROM THEM THE THINGS THEY NEED..
BUT THE HARDEST PRISON TO ESCAPE ...
---IS THE ONE WHER WE ARE GIVEN EVERYTHIN WE WANT.

THE ECLIPSE ESCAPIST

by catherine yronwode

ECLIPSE COMICS WAS A SMALL BUT FEISTY INDEPENDENT COMIC BOOK publisher founded by the brothers Jan and Dean Mullaney in the late 1970s. As Dean saw it, the company's mission was to promote the legal rights of creators and to provide them with the high production values he felt were commensurate with the effort they brought to their art.

By the time i came on board as an editor at Eclipse in the early 1980s, the company had moved from black-and-white to colour production and was gaining a lot of attention for its iconoclastic attitude.

During the time i worked for Eclipse, the company's emphasis on adult-oriented naturalism was displayed in a number of ways. Most shocking to the public were probably the books that dealt with human physiology — a story in which Charles Vess drew a girl with her first menstrual blood dripping down her leg, an issue of *Sabre* in which the lead female protagonist gave birth to twins on panel, and the celebrated issue of *Miracleman* in which the hero's wife also had a baby in full view of the reader's gaze. But Eclipse's iconoclasm ran far deeper than those highly visible presentations of women's reproductive issues. Many of the staff members had a left-wing political bent and had been active in local and national politics all of their lives, in particular the civil rights struggle and the peace movement of the Vietnam War era. To us, Eclipse Comics was a "bully pulpit" from which we could preach our own beliefs in the form of non-fiction "docu-comics." And why not? Didn't Archie, Marvel, and DC also preach their own political values in their heroic fiction comics? Of course they did.

Among the non-fiction political comics and trading cards Eclipse published — often at a loss, which was underwritten by other, more middle-of-the-road superhero ventures — were such presentations as *Brought to Light*, a graphic novel about the CIA; "Coup D'Etat," a set of trading cards about the Kennedy assassination; and *Real War Stories*, a series of comics designed to take the mystique and mystery out of military combat by displaying it in all its immoral depravity.

Issue #1 of *RWS* was produced as an outreach project with the Central Committee for Conscientious Objectors, an anti-war organization, and issue #2 was created in conjunction with Citizen Soldier, a soldiers' legal rights group. Although the first issue wasn't published until 1987, the series actually began production four years earlier, in 1983, for reasons having to do with lengthy and complicated approval procedures. The stories were all factual, and although some were historical in nature, others drew from firsthand interviews with living veterans of various wars.

The story you are about to read was originally one such factual narrative, told by a Vietnam War vet named Don Roach, whom Dean and i knew because he lived in our own small town of Forestville, California. Tom Yeates, who had worked on the first issue of *Real War Stories* and would subsequently illustrate half of *Brought to Light*, was chosen to draw this piece as well, because he likes to work from living models whenever he can, and Don agreed to let himself be photographed for use as "reference."

Don's memoir, "Take No Prisoners," was a blunt, brutally ugly examination of the horrors he had experienced firsthand. There was no "Escapist" in his tale, and, in fact, the entire piece was simply a monologue about how a young boy of seventeen, fresh from working on his grandfather's asparagus farm near Santa Rosa, had volunteered to fight for his country, became a radio operator during President Nixon's "secret war" in Cambodia and Laos, and had been made to take part in scenes of carnage, death, and destruction on a scale he could not have imagined.

The completed story was originally slated to appear in the second issue of *Real War Stories* — the last ever to see print, as things would turn out. However, within a few months, we had a new plan for the story — and one that no one expected: Eclipse was suddenly approached by Omnigrip, a large development corporation, with a proposal for a joint venture, a 120-page graphic novel featuring the Escapist, a character which Omnigrip controlled but had made little use of at the time.

THE ECLIPSE ESCAPIST

Apparently the powers-that-be at Omnigrip were so impressed with our upstart publishing company that they were willing to bring the Escapist to the table for a one-shot, just to see if we could manage to pull off a successful revival of the character,[1] thus paving the way for future licensing deals in presumably more lucrative fields, like television or movies.

The trouble was, Omnigrip wanted us to jump three hurdles on our way to working with them.

First, although they would grant us the rights to use the Escapist for the one co-produced graphic novel, we had to pay for production of all the work ourselves in lieu of a licensing fee.

Second, they wanted the first 22-page chapter of the book impossibly quickly: within a week!

Third — and i am quoting from a memo here — they wanted a "realistic, political, iconoclastic story that would generate controversial publicity, like on *Larry King Live* or *Montel Williams*."

Boy, did i have a story for them!

With Don Roach's permission, i hired Chris Offutt, a non-comics author who had sent me some great writing samples, to completely re-script Don's true tale of what it was like being over the border when Nixon gave his famous speech proclaiming that there were no U.S. troops on the ground in Cambodia or Laos. I then got Tom back for the day or so it took him to redraw the lead character as the Escapist. Don Roach's narrator character had made heavy use of weaponry, as was only to be expected, and all of that had to be whited out when the story was remade as fiction, for, as everyone knows, the Escapist does not use guns or knives.

We got the whole thing rewritten and redrawn — and then relettered by Tom Orzechowski — in less than a week, turned it in to the folks at Omnigrip ... and waited.

And waited.

Eventually they called back. They had changed their minds. The Escapist graphic novel was off. "Too controversial," they said. They paid us a ten-thousand-dollar kill-fee for our work on the project, and we kicked most of the money back to Don, Chris, and Tom. i still figured we could use that story in an upcoming issue of *Real War Stories* — Tom could again redraw the Escapist character, who, after all, never appeared in costume — when i got the news that the entire Eclipse staff, myself included, was being laid off. Less than a month later, Eclipse went bankrupt. As the last person in the office — Dean had split for New York with his new girlfriend — i made a unilateral decision to return all of the in-house projects to whoever had drawn them. Tom came out and picked up the *Real War/Escapist* art himself. He and i hoisted a beer with Don Roach, who was doing some carpentry work for me at the time, and we shook our heads and laughed a little over the old days at Eclipse.

Luckily, Tom held onto the story until the wheel of fortune took another spin. Omnigrip eventually lost its hold on the Escapist,[2] and now, more than twenty years after it was first created, the public can at last see this fine little glimpse of political realism — fictionalized, of course, but nonetheless still a "real war story" at heart.

Catherine Yronwode works in the production department of Claypool Comics and is the proprietor of The Lucky Mojo Curio Company, a manufactory of occult and spiritual supplies located in the old Eclipse offices in Forestville, California, which you can view on the web at <http://www.luckymojo.com/mojocatphotos.html>.

---

[1] Perhaps not coincidentally, Eclipse would later establish a reputation for resurrecting second-rank out-of-work heroes — like Airboy, Skywolf, the Black Terror, and Miracleman — and catapulting them into contemporary popularity.

[2] In fact, it was less than a year later, in 1984, that Omnigrip sold off all the old Empire characters, including the Escapist, to their previous owner Danny Sonnenschein, at a bargain price.

1972.
VIETNAM.
NEAR THE CAMBODIA BORDER.
HOT LZ. HOT LZ. LANDING IMPOSSIBLE. OVER.
DUMP THE CARGO AND RETURN. REPEAT-- DUMP THE CARGO.

ANOTHER MAN'S ESCAPE
CARGO AWAY. CARGO AWAY. OVER.

RETURN TO BASE. REPEAT. RETURN TO BASE. YOU'RE DONE.
STORY BY CHRIS OFFUTT ART BY THOMAS YEATES

THE BIGGEST ESCAPE I EVER MADE IS THE ONE I FEEL WORST ABOUT.
THE GOVERNMENT GAVE ME A SPECIAL DEFERMENT FOR MY SERVICES AGAINST CRIME IN THE STATES.
BUT I NEVER FELT GOOD ABOUT ESCAPING THE DRAFT.
NO ONE FELT GOOD ABOUT VIETNAM.

I PULLED SOME STRINGS AND GOT A SSION. PROBABLY THE NLY MAN WHO USED LITICAL CONNECTIONS TO GO *TO* THIS WAR.
DEFINITELY THE ONL MAN WITHOUT A *GUN*.
EVEN THE *MEDICS* CARRIED A PISTOL.
BUT I SWORE BY THE KEY TO NEVER CARRY A WEAPON. NEVER TAKE A LIFE.

DOING EITHER MAKES ME THE SAME AS THE PEOPLE I SWORE TO FIGHT.

STILL, I FELT VULNERABLE AS A MOUSE.

ESPECIALLY WHEN FACING AN M-16 LOCKED AND LOADED FOR FULL-TILT BOOGIE ROCK-'N'-ROLL.
PRIVATE TOM MAYFLOWER REPORTING FOR DUTY.
I'M LIEUTENANT SAMUELS.
DON'T BOTHER SALUTING-- WE'RE TOO FAR IN THE BOONIES FOR THAT. BESIDES, YOU'RE NOT MILITARY. THAT LEAVES SNEAKY PETE* OR C.I.A., BUT YOU'RE UNARMED.
SO JUST WHAT IS IT THAT YOU WANT IN MY LITTLE KINGDOM OF MUD?
*G.I. SLANG FOR SPECIAL FORCES.

SIR, MY ORDERS ARE TO ASSIST IN THE *LIBERATION* OF AMERICAN PRISONERS OF WAR.
THEY SENT *YOU*, HUH? THE *COMPANY* RECRUIT YOU STRAIGHT OUT OF THE IVY LEAGUES?
ARE YOU A *ONE-MAN ARMY?* SOME KIND OF *KUNG-FU CHAMPION* BACK IN THE WORLD?
I'M A *CONCERNED* CITIZEN, SIR. A *PATRIOT.*
I DON'T NEED PATRIOTS. I NEED *MEDICAL* SUPPLIES. I NEED *AMMUNITION* AND *RATIONS.*
AN UNARMED MAN I NEED LIKE A *HOLE* IN THE HEAD--
--AND YOU NEVER KNOW, IT MIGHT HAPPEN *TODAY.*

WHERE IS THE P.O.W. CAMP?
SOMEWHERE IN CAMBODIA.

BUT WE'RE NOT AT WAR WITH CAMBODIA.
BORDERS DON'T MEAN THE SAME HERE.

THOSE BOYS NEVER CROSSED THE DOPE BORDER BEFORE THEY CAME HERE.

ARE YOU GOING TO HELP ME OR NOT?

THERE'S THE ONLY MAN WHO CAN HELP.
CORPORAL JAMES SURVIVED AN AMBUSH THAT KILLED ELEVEN MEN. THREE MORE WERE CAPTURED.

JAMES CAME BACK COVERED IN BLOOD, WITH A MACHETE AND A THOUSAND-YARD STARE.

HE WON'T TALK ABOUT IT.

NOT ALL CASUALTIES OF WAR ARE DEAD.

CORPORAL JAMES WAS AS UNARMED AS ME.
BUT HIS *SILENCE* WAS A WEAPON.
A WEAPON I UNDERSTOOD. THE LONELY STRUGGLE WITH ONESELF.
LIFE BACK THEN WAS CRAZY, WITHOUT RULES OR REASON.
Corporal James
Zachary James
717 Cherry Way
Riverside, Iowa
HIS RESPONSE MADE MORE SENSE THAN MINE.
Corporal James
Mr. Will E. James
717 Cherry way
Riverside, Iowa
Riverside, Iowa
Riverside, Iowa

CORPORAL JAMES?
OUI.
AH, VOUS ÊTES FRANÇAIS?
NO, ARE YOU?
NO, I'M FROM EMPIRE CITY.
HOW'S THE MAIL SERVICE THERE?
PRETTY GOOD. WHO ARE THESE LETTERS TO?
EVERYBODY IN MY HOMETOWN.
NEED HELP MAILING THEM OFF?
I DON'T NEED *NOTHING.*

THAT'S HOW HE COPES. YOU'LL HAVE TO HELP HIM ESCAPE IT BEFORE HE'LL TALK.
ANY IDEAS?

EVERY NIGHT THE V.C. TAUNT US OVER A P.A. SYSTEM. NO PATROL CAN FIND WHERE THEY OPERATE.

JAMES HATES IT. ALWAYS HAS.

WHAT'S YOUR WAY OF ESCAPING THE WAR?

WHAT WAR?
AT MIDNIGHT I CARRIED THE FIGHT TO THE ENEMY. HOPING TO LIBERATE CORPORAL JAMES FROM HIMSELF.
I WAS HERE TO ESCAPE MY GUILT OVER AVOIDING THE DRAFT. BUT THE VIET CONG SAW THINGS DIFFERENTLY.
YOU ARE NOTHING, G.I.
GIVE UP, G.I.
THEIR ONLY ESCAPE WAS THE WAR ITSELF.
YOUR MOTHER HATES YOU.
YOUR GIRLFRIEND LEFT YOU.
THEY HAD NOTHING TO LOSE.
GO HOME, G.I.
WE HAD NOTHING TO GAIN.

THE AK-47 IS THE BEST GUN EVER MADE.
SO GOO AT KILLIN THAT ITS INVENTO WAS ASHAME
BUT IN HAND-TO-HAND COMBAT...
...A RIFLE IS JUST A STICK WITH HANDLES.
AND A MEGAPHONE IS LANGUAGE WITH A PISTOL-GRIP.

A SUCCESSFUL ARMY RELIES ON TRAINING, DISCIPLINE, SUPPLY LINES, INTELLIGENCE REPORTS, AIR STRIKES, COMMUNICATION...
CORPORAL JAMES! I BRING YOU GREETINGS FROM HOME.
...TROOP STRENGTH, ARMOR, RATIONS, AND AMMO.
JEFF SAYS HELLO. SCOTTY AND MISSY, TOO.
BUT INDIVIDUAL SOLDIERS NEED MORALE.
THE GIRLS STILL PUT THEIR JEANS ON WET AND LET THEM DRY.
AND I NEEDED TO KNOW THE LOCATION OF THE PRISONERS.
THE BOYS STILL COMB THEIR HAIR WITH WATER AT THE SOCK HOP.
US ARMY

THEY'RE STILL PLAYING BASEBALL BY TRUCK HEADLIGHT AT NIGHT IN THE LOWER FORTY.
EVERY-BODY MISSES YOU.
IT'LL BE A GREAT YEAR FOR THE CROPS.
READY TO MOVE OUT, CORPORAL?
YES, SIR!

AMBODIA.
WITH CORPORAL JAMES FREED FROM THE PRISON OF HIS MIND, I WAS NO LONGER ALONE AND UNARMED.
BUT I DIDN'T FEEL RIGHT ABOUT HELPING HIM ESCAPE HIS OWN ESCAPE.

BECAUSE NOW HE WAS A WEAPON I'D CLEANED AND OILED...
V.C. NO GOOD!

...AND UNLEASHED IN THE JUNGLE.

WHILE HE DREW FIRE, I FLANKED THE ENEMY.
AND DID THE ONLY THING I'M GOOD AT.
LEAVING HIM SURROUNDED AT TERRIBLE ODDS.
I COULD HEAR BURSTS OF AUTOMATIC RIFLES IN A FIREFIGHT, GIVING THE PRISONERS AND ME A ROUTE OF ESCAPE.

MAYBE CORPORAL JAMES WAS BETTER OFF TETHERED TO A TREE. MAYBE IT WASN'T *VIETNAM* HE WANTED TO ESCAPE. MAYBE IT WAS THE KNOWLEDGE OF HOW GOOD HE'D BECOME AT *KILLING*.
BUT THE FLIP SIDE WAS LEARNING HOW MUCH HE WANTED TO *LIVE*.

For corporal James, this mission was about more than freeing the prisoners.
It was about making sure no G.I.s would ever be imprisoned here again.
It was about defeating *all* his enemies.
G.I. number one!
No man left behind!

I UNDERSTOOD WHY CORPORAL JAMES NEEDED THE ESCAPE I'D FREED HIM FROM.
I KNEW WHY LIEUTENANT SAMUELS ACCEPTED IT.
RADIO A MEDEVAC.
OUTSTANDING WORK, CORPORAL. GLAD TO HAVE YOU BACK.
THANK YOU, SIR.
AS FOR YOU--

I'D SERVED MY COUNTRY. BUT NOT CORPORAL JAMES.
--CUP O COFFEE?
HE'D DONE MY KILLING FOR ME.

I'D KEPT MY OATH TO THE KEY...
HOW DO *YOU* ESCAPE THIS WAR?
I DON'T.
THIS IS WHERE I ESCAPED *TO.*

...BUT NO ONE ESCAPES WAR WITHOUT BLOOD ON HIS HANDS.

THE "ESCAPIST"

RATTLE

RATTLE
SHAKE
ROLL

jason

Weird DATE

SEPTEMBER, 1949

10¢

WAS HE THE
MAN OF HER
DREAMS...
OR THE
START OF A
NIGHTMARE?!

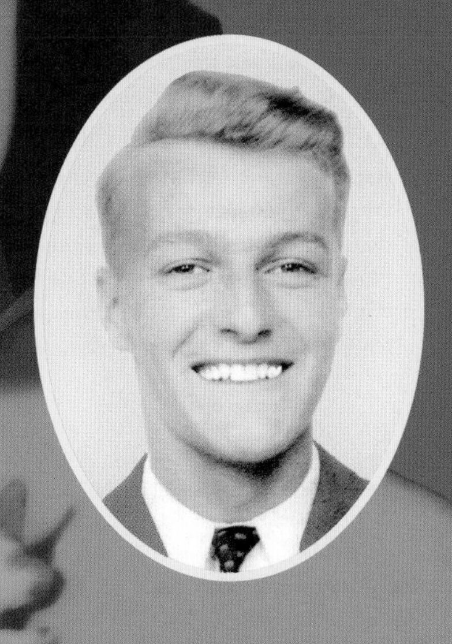

WEIRD DATE

by Bubbles LaTour

WITH THE END OF WORLD WAR II, AMERICA'S LOVE OF SUPERHEROES began its first slow death (not to be resurrected until the later '50s with the advent of the Silver Age reinvention of the genre). In an effort to stay in business, comics publishers began experimenting with different types of stories: horror, science fiction, war, crime, and more. Then, in 1947, *Captain America* creators Joe Simon and Jack Kirby introduced the very first love comic: *Young Romance.* It was a raging success.

Combining teen date concepts, such as *Archie* had made popular, with the confessional tone of the old romance pulps, *Young Romance* spawned countless imitators. By 1952, there were 527 different romance comics titles being published.[1]

Heretofore ignored by the industry, the primary readers of romance comics were women. And the stories themselves focused on women. But despite the fact that the three S&K titles — *Young Romance, Young Love,* and *Young Brides* — were supposedly told from the first-person perspective of a female narrator, all were actually authored by men.[2]

Until, that is, Rosa Saks came along, paving the way for more women to enter the field (such as romance comics publisher Ruth "Ray" Hermann, among others).

Following what proved a futile attempt at more "serious" writing, and with a wife and child to support, *Escapist* co-creator Sam Clay had returned to the world of comics in 1947 as editor-in-chief of Gold Star Publications. After clearing out the less than competent members of Gold Star's staff, Sam was left with a shortage of artists. So he hired his wife Rosa to write and draw a *Young Romance* imitation, *Working Gals* — whose banner advertised "shocking but true tales from the fevered lives of career girls." In subsequent years, Rosa followed up *Working Gals* with such titles as *Heartache, Sweetheart,* and *Kiss,* earning for herself — or, rather, for "Rose Saxon" — the title of Queen of Romance Comics.

Meanwhile, Sam created his own peculiar take on the romance genre with *Weird Date.* An odd blend of genres — romance and crime, romance and horror — the title, a reflection of Clay's own ambiguous feelings about his marriage, was a runaway best-seller nonetheless. It is said that Joe Kavalier himself, who was in hiding during those years completing his magnum opus *The Golem,* never missed reading an issue.

The *Weird Date* story that follows, "Electricity," first saw print in 1949 and featured, as was standard for the time, the photo cover reproduced on the previous page. While, with rare exceptions, artists did not begin receiving actual credit until the 1960s, certain comics art historians attribute this story to Alex Toth, whose work on Famous Funnies' *Personal Love* shows distinct similarities. However, the frenzied layouts of the last half of the story are more suggestive of Jack Cole's style as evinced in the pages of *True Crime* and *Crime Does Not Pay.* While the actual artist may forever remain unknown, the story itself springs unmistakably from the tortured soul of Sam Clay.

---

[1] Howell, Richard, ed. From his introduction. *Real Love: The Best of the Simon and Kirby Romance Comics.* Forestville, CA: Eclipse Books, 1988: pg. 8.

[2] Simon, Joe, with Jim Simon. *The Comic Book Makers.* New York, NY: Crestwood/II Publications, 1990: pg. 123.

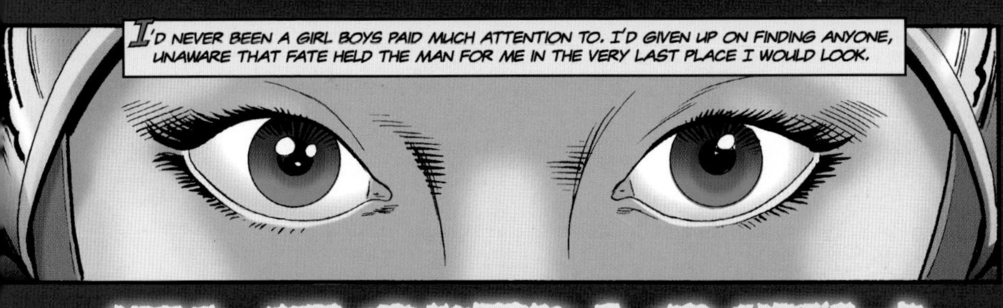

I'D NEVER BEEN A GIRL BOYS PAID MUCH ATTENTION TO. I'D GIVEN UP ON FINDING ANYONE, UNAWARE THAT FATE HELD THE MAN FOR ME IN THE VERY LAST PLACE I WOULD LOOK.

ELECTRICITY

A BLIND DATE? WHY WOULD HE WANT ME?
LISTEN, ELLIE, BOB SAYS HE'S JUST YOUR TYPE. HE HAS SOME SORT OF GOVERNMENT JOB...

I SHOULD HAVE TOLD SUSAN I DIDN'T NEED HER CHARITY. BUT SHE MEANT WELL, AND I WAS LONELY...

IS IT TRUE? OUR LITTLE ELLIE'S GOING OUT ON A DATE?
WELL, SHE HASN'T SAID SO YET.

THEN THE OFFICE BUSYBODIES GOT WIND OF IT.

OH, OF COURSE YOU WILL, ELLIE! BUT YOU'LL NEVER GET A MAN LOOKING LIKE THAT!
YOU LET US GET YOU READY, DEAR. WE KNOW WHAT MEN LIKE.

THEY WERE LIKE CHILDREN PLAYING WITH A NEW DOLL, FAIRY GODMOTHERS FUSSING OVER A CAPTIVE CINDERELLA.
I WANTED TO SCREAM. WHO WERE THEY, TO REMAKE ME?

THEY WERE WOMEN WHO HAD ALREADY WON THEIR MEN. ADMITTING IT ACHED, BUT IT WAS TRUE.
MY MOTHER ALWAYS TOLD ME BOYS DIDN'T LIKE GIRLS WHO PUSHED, SO I'D BEEN TIMID AROUND THEM, WAITING FOR THEM TO NOTICE ME.
JEFFERS HIGH SCHO
THEY DIDN'T.
CASABLANC
MY MOTHER SAID I WAS A LATE BLOOMER, AND I'D BLOSSOM IN TIME.
I DIDN'T.
BUT ALL AROUND ME WERE REMINDERS OF WHAT I WAS SUPPOSED TO HAVE, WHAT I SHOULD HAVE HAD.
DID I GIVE UP? DID I TAKE A JOB THAT WOULD MAKE ME INVISIBLE JUST SO I WOULDN'T HAVE TO TRY?
MY MOTHER TAUGHT ME INNER BEAUTY WAS ENOUGH. BUT IT WASN'T. IT WASN'T.
IT WASN'T ENOUGH FOR ME!
THAT'S WHY I SAID NOTHING, WHY I LET THE OFFICE WOMEN DO WHAT THEY LIKED, WITHOUT COMPLAINT.
I WANTED, FOR ONCE IN MY LIFE, TO BE DESIRED.

I WANTED TO BE BEAUTIFUL OUTSIDE, TOO.
AND I WAS.

ON MY WAY TO THE DATE, I CAUGHT THE CABBIE EYEING ME. I SAID NOTHING. I'D NEVER BEEN EYED BEFORE.
IT WAS A STRANGE, STRANGE EXPERIENCE, REPELLENT BUT EXCITING.

AT THE RESTAURANT, ALL THE MEN-- EVEN THE MEN WITH OTHER WOMEN!-- WERE LOOKING AT ME!
IT WAS SO BIZARRE AND WONDERFUL. FOR THE FIRST TIME IN MY LIFE, I FELT CONFIDENT THIS MAN, WHOEVER HE WAS, WOULD LOVE ME.

BUT TWENTY MINUTES PASSED, AND HE WASN'T THERE. I WAS SO AFRAID HE WASN'T COMING. OR, WORSE, THAT HE'D BEEN THERE, AND SEEN ME, AND LEFT.
THE MEN OGLING ME, AND EVEN THEIR SCORN-FUL DATES, NOW LOOKED AWAY UNCOMFORTABLY, EYES FILLED WITH THAT HORRID PITY THAT HAD DOGGED ME ALL MY LIFE.

HERE. COMPLIMENTS OF THE HOUSE. WHILE YOU'RE WAITING, I MEAN.
DON'T THINK TWICE ABOUT HIM, HONEY. THERE'S ALWAYS ANOTHER ONE.

BUT THE DARK VOICE IN MY HEAD TOLD ME THERE WOULDN'T BE, NOT FOR ME.
I NEVER DRANK, BUT AS THE MINUTES TORTUROUSLY TICKED ON, IT WAS SOMETHING TO DO WITH MY HANDS...

WHAT WERE THEY THINKING?
DID THEY REALLY THINK I COULD BECOME INTERESTED IN SOME SLUTTY ALCOHOLIC?
ARE YOU... ARE YOU... EDWARD?

HE WAS BEAUTIFUL, EVERYTHING I'D EVER WANTED IN A MAN. ALL HE'D DONE WAS GET THE TIME WRONG. I'D RUINED EVERYTHING WITH MY FOOLISH PANIC.
I WANTED TO CATCH HIM, EXPLAIN, WIN HIS LOVE-- HE'D LISTEN-- I KNEW WE WERE MEANT TO BE!

THEN MY LEGS SHOOK. MY HEAD POUNDED.
SOMETHING WARM AND BITTER, TASTING OF SOUR WINE, BURNED UP INTO MY THROAT.
MY STOMACH BETRAYED ME!

AND HE WAS GONE, AND THERE WAS NOTHING I COULD DO ABOUT IT.
WOW, YOU'RE IN BAD SHAPE, SWEETIE. LET ME HOLD YOUR HAIR FOR YOU.

HER NAME WAS ALICE. SHE WAS NICE.
MAYBE IT WAS THE WINE, MAYBE I JUST NEEDED TO TALK, BUT I FOUND MYSELF TELLING HER EVERYTHING.

HE SOUNDS LIKE A CREEP TO ME, SWEETIE, AND I KNOW CREEPS. YOU CAN DO BETTER.
A CAR'S WAITING FOR ME. COME ON, WE'LL GET YOU HOME.
MAYBE THAT WAS THE WINE, TOO. OR MAYBE I KNEW WHAT WAS COMING. MAYBE I WAS TRYING TO PUNISH MYSELF.

Ritz RESTAURANT
RESTAURANT
MAYBE. MAYBE.
IT ALL SOUNDS SO STUPID NOW.
WHO'S YOUR FRIEND?
LEAVE HER ALONE, TOMMY. SHE'S HAD TOO MUCH TO DRINK.
YEAH? THEN SHE'S JUST MY TYPE.
HERE, YOU DRIVE.
PHEW! SURE CAN'T HOLD YOUR LIQUOR, CAN YOU?
HE WAS A PIG. I KNOW THAT. BUT DON'T JUDGE ME.
DON'T YOU JUDGE ME!
HE WASN'T MUCH, BUT HE WAS THERE!
WHAT'S THE PROBLEM? I GOT SOMETHING ON MY FACE?
YOU'RE ACTING AWFUL FUNNY...
HE WAS THERE, AND HE WANTED ME!
SOMEONE WANTED ME!

I HATED HIM, AND HOW HIS BREATH WHISTLED BETWEEN HIS TEETH, AND THE BURNING STENCH OF HIS CHEAP COLOGNE.
I LOVED HIS BURNING FINGERTIPS, HOW MY SKIN TINGLED WHEREVER HE TOUCHED ME.
MY HEAD SWAM. MY BODY WAS SOMEWHERE ELSE. I WAS SWALLOWED UP, DROWNING IN A POOL OF DARK FIRE.
I DIDN'T WANT TO BREATHE.
I DIDN'T TRY TO BREATHE.
I DON'T REMEMBER WHAT HAPPENED AFTER THAT.
I DON'T WANT TO KNOW WHAT HAPPENED.
I DON'T EVER WANT TO KNOW.

BUT I KNEW I'D RUINED EVERYTHING.
I WANT TO GO HOME...
COOL IT, BABY. WE WON'T BE BUT A MINUTE. GET YOU A PINT OF ANYTHING?
I'M NOT YOUR BABY...
EVERYONE'S MY BABY, BABY.
WHO WOULD WANT ME NOW?
I WANTED EDWARD. I WANTED HIM MORE THAN I'D EVER WANTED ANYTHING.
BUT HE WOULDN'T WANT ME. NOT NOW. NO MAN WOULD EVER WANT ME AGAIN.
EVERY SECOND WAS ANOTHER BADGE OF SHAME. WHAT WAS TAKING THEM SO LONG?
WHERE WERE THEY?

I JUST WANTED THE NIGHT TO END! I JUST WANTED TO GO HOME!
THEN I REALIZED--

THEY DIDN'T KNOW WHERE I LIVED! THEY DIDN'T KNOW WHO I WAS! I COULD MAKE THE WHOLE NIGHT A BAD DREAM!
WHOEVER THEY WERE, WHATEVER THEY WERE DOING, I HAD NOTHING TO DO WITH IT!
THAT WAS WHEN I HEARD FATE LAUGHING BEHIND MY BACK.
LIQUOR
TOMMMEEEE!
BOOM
THINK YOU'RE TOUGH?
BLAM
YOU'RE A QUICK STUDY! GO! GO! GO! GO! GO!
WE... WE CAN'T JUST... WHAT ABOUT HIM? WHAT ABOUT ALICE?
OWW!
WHAT ABOUT HER?
DRIVE!
SLAP
I SHOULDN'T HAVE, BUT HE HAD A GUN. I WAS SCARED. EVERYTHING WAS SO HORRIBLY OUT OF CONTROL.
AND HE JUST. WOULDN'T. SHUT. UP.
MAN! THERE MUST BE A THOUSAND BUCKS HERE!

ARREEEEEE
WHAT? HOW DID THEY--?
#%@&! THAT KID MUST'VE TRIPPED A SILENT ALARM!
PUT SOME SPEED INTO IT, BABY!
VRROOOM
I WANTED TO SCREAM, BUT I COULDN'T. I COULDN'T SCREAM. THERE WAS NOWHERE FOR IT TO GO.
IT WOULD DIE WITH ME, AND NO ONE WOULD EVER KNOW...
WE'LL NEVER MAKE IT! YOU'LL GET THE CHAIR FOR WHAT YOU DID!
NOT IN THIS STATE, NOT UNLESS YOU KILL A COP! DOESN'T MATTER ANYWAY!
NO WAY THEY'RE GETTING US, BABY!
NO WAY I'M EVER GOING INSIDE AGAIN!
BLAM
HE WAS INSANE!
AND WHAT WAS I? A STUPID, TIMID LITTLE GIRL WHO'D NEVER GROWN UP, WHO'D WASTED HER LIFE PLAYING IT SAFE...
BLAM
BLAM
SOMETHING JUMPED IN FRONT OF US-- I COULDN'T STOP-- WE WERE GOING TOO FAST--

THE WHOLE SKY WENT FUNNY COLORS...
SKAASH
WHAM
SOMEHOW I WAS OUT OF THE CAR. IT WAS RAINING. IT WAS MY BLOOD. SOMEHOW TOMMY WAS OUT, TOO, HOWLING LIKE AN ANIMAL...
COME ON! COME AND GET ME! COME ON!
HE JUST WOULDN'T SHUT UP.
BLAM
klik klik klik
HA! YOU'RE ONE SLOW COP, COP.
THAT'S ALL HE HAD TO DO. THAT'S ALL I WANTED.
GIMME THE GUN, BABY! C'MON, HURRY UP!
YOU LISTENING TO ME?
I DIDN'T KNOW WHAT WAS GOING ON. THE WHOLE WORLD WAS DROWNED OUT BY HIS VOICE.
HIS DISGUSTING, DISGUSTING VOICE!
GIMME THE #%@&* GUN!
WHY COULDN'T HE JUST SHUT UP?

SHUT UP.
BLAM
SHUT UP.
BLAM
BLAM
SHUT UP!
BLAM
BLAM
BLAM
BLAM
THAT WAS HOW I FOUND THE PERFECT MAN AND LOST EVERYTHING.

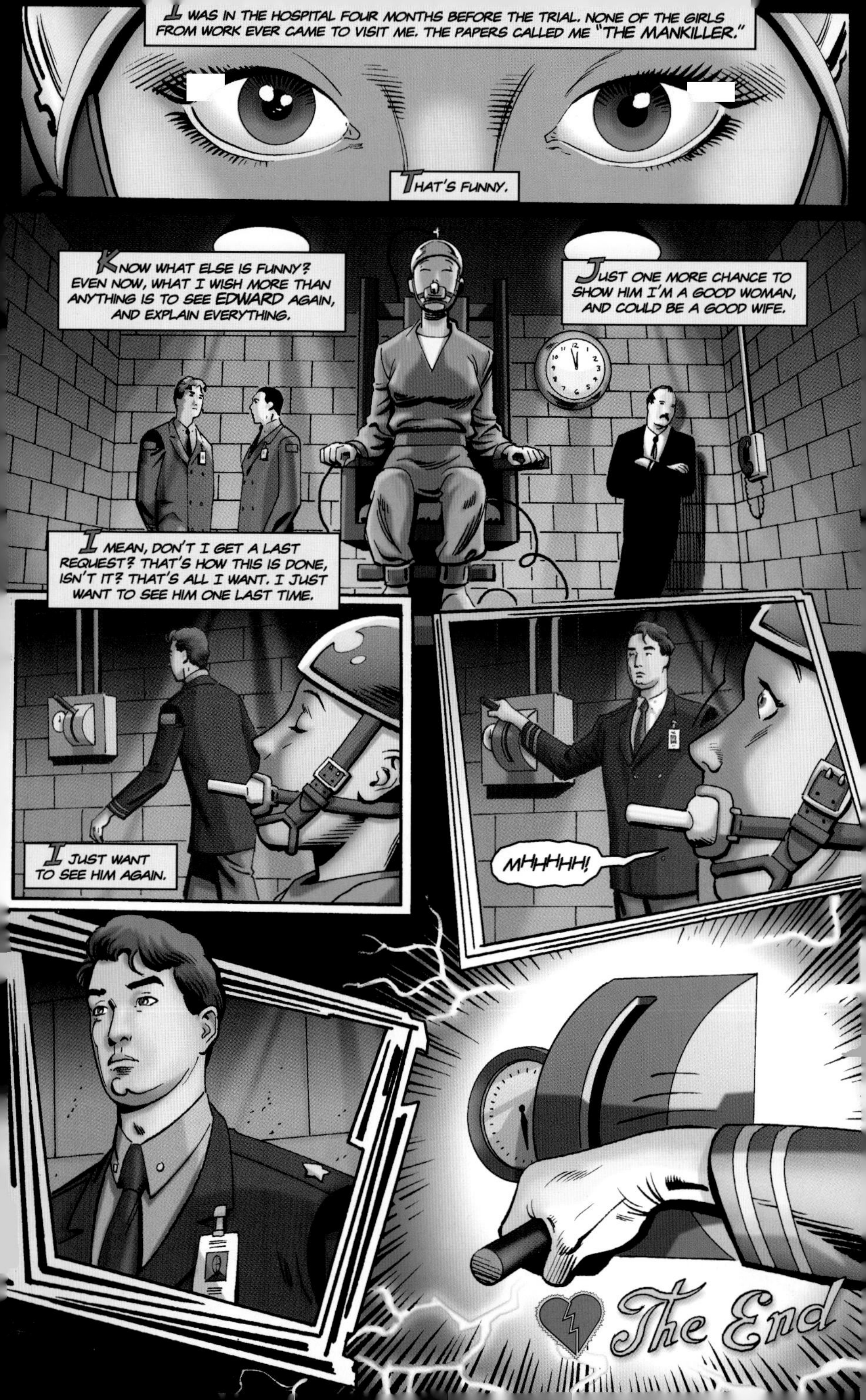
I WAS IN THE HOSPITAL FOUR MONTHS BEFORE THE TRIAL. NONE OF THE GIRLS FROM WORK EVER CAME TO VISIT ME. THE PAPERS CALLED ME "THE MANKILLER."
THAT'S FUNNY.
KNOW WHAT ELSE IS FUNNY? EVEN NOW, WHAT I WISH MORE THAN ANYTHING IS TO SEE EDWARD AGAIN, AND EXPLAIN EVERYTHING.
JUST ONE MORE CHANCE TO SHOW HIM I'M A GOOD WOMAN, AND COULD BE A GOOD WIFE.
I MEAN, DON'T I GET A LAST REQUEST? THAT'S HOW THIS IS DONE, ISN'T IT? THAT'S ALL I WANT. I JUST WANT TO SEE HIM ONE LAST TIME.
I JUST WANT TO SEE HIM AGAIN.
MHHHHH!
The End

THE GREEKS HAD A WORD FOR IT...
...NO, NOT FOR THAT, YOU NASTY, DIRTY LITTLE CREATURE...
THEY CALLED THEM SIRENS--DROP-DEAD GORGEOUS DREAMBOATS WHO LURED MEN TO THEIR DOOM WITH SONG...
...AND--
the ESCAPIST
--IS IN FOR THE SAME TREATMENT, UNLESS HE CAN LIFT THE NEEDLE ON--
THE SIREN SONG OF CIRCE O'SHAUGHNESSY!
WRITTEN BY HOWARD "HOPHEAD" CHAYKIN
ILLUSTRATED, COLORED, AND LETTERED BY DAVID "DIZZY" HAHN
EDITED BY DIANA "DIG YOU LATER" SCHUTZ

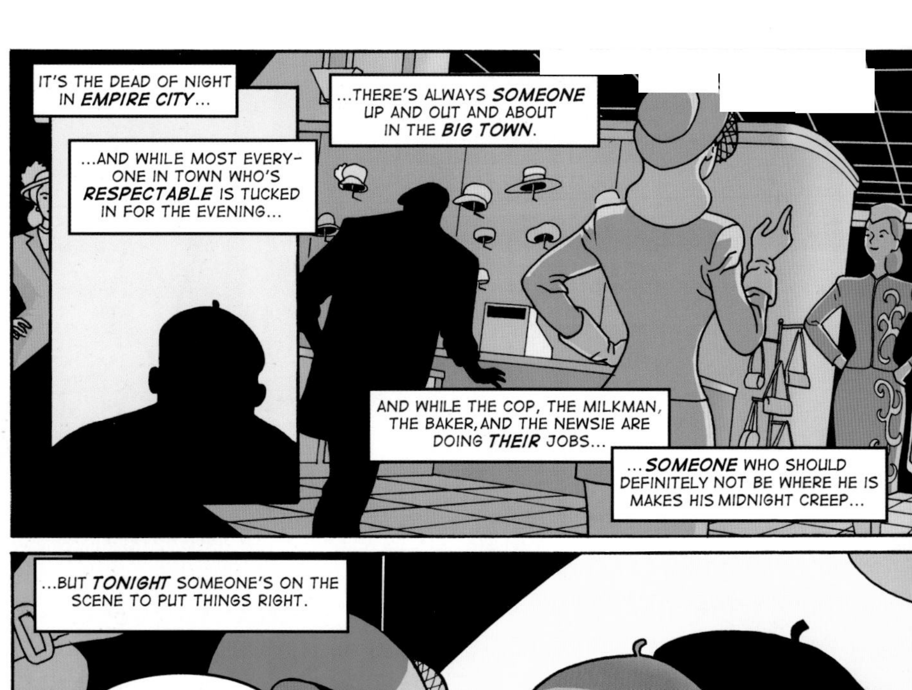
IT'S THE DEAD OF NIGHT IN EMPIRE CITY...
...AND WHILE MOST EVERY-ONE IN TOWN WHO'S RESPECTABLE IS TUCKED IN FOR THE EVENING...
...THERE'S ALWAYS SOMEONE UP AND OUT AND ABOUT IN THE BIG TOWN.
AND WHILE THE COP, THE MILKMAN, THE BAKER, AND THE NEWSIE ARE DOING THEIR JOBS...
...SOMEONE WHO SHOULD DEFINITELY NOT BE WHERE HE IS MAKES HIS MIDNIGHT CREEP...

...BUT TONIGHT SOMEONE'S ON THE SCENE TO PUT THINGS RIGHT.
HOLD IT RIGHT THERE, BIG FELLA...
HUH?!
WHERE AM I?
WHO AM I?
WE GOT ANOTHER ONE--
--THAT MAKES THREE SLEEPWALKING SECOND-STORY ARTISTS THIS WEEK.

...AND SEVERAL HUNDRED DOLLARS IN BAIL BONDS *LATER*...
WHAT *HAPPENED* TO ME, OMAR?
IT WOULD SEEM YOU WERE *HYPNOTIZED*, ALOIS...
RIDICULOUS.
NO ONE'S *EVER* BEEN ABLE TO HYPNOTIZE M--
IT WOULD SEEM THAT ALOIS'S *LIMITED* SELF-AWARENESS GOES FAR DEEPER THAN WE MIGHT HAVE *BELIEVED*, TOM.
BE *GENTLE* WITH AL, PLUM...
...BEING OUT ON *BAIL* FOR BREAKING AND ENTERING'S TOUGH *ENOUGH* ON THE BIG GUY AS IT *IS*.
AND IF YOU WILL *BOTH* KINDLY REMAIN *SILENT*...
...*PERHAPS* WE WILL BE ABLE TO LEARN *PRECISELY* WHAT BIG AL WAS *DOING* IN THAT DEPARTMENT STORE LAST NIGHT.
THE *LAST* THING I REMEMBER...
...I WAS ENTRANCED AND *ENCHANTED*...

"...HEY, WAIT A MINUTE-- FORGET ABOUT ENCHANTED...
"...I WAS DIGGING AND WIGGING TO SOME SOLID SOUNDS ON TEMPO STREET...
"...AT A CELLAR JOINT KNOWN AS BOP 'TIL YOU DROP CITY...
"...SOUNDS THAT WERE TOO COOL FROM A FINE FRAIL WHO WAS DEFINITELY HOT...
"...BY THE NAME OF CIRCE O'SHAUGHNESSY.
"I'D NEVER HEARD ANYBODY BLOW ADOLPH SAX'S GIFT TO MODERN JAZZ WITH SUCH ABANDONED APLOMB...
"...LET ALONE SO PETITE A SKIRT AS CIRCE."

"DIGGING--WIGGING --FRAIL--SKIRT?"
"SILENCE, *PLEASE*...!
"...GO *ON*, ALOIS..."
"WITHOUT *WARNING*, THE MUSIC SUDDENLY SEEMED TO CLIMB *THROUGH* MY EARS INTO MY VERY *HEAD*...
"...AS CIRCE'S *IMPROVISATION* BRUTALLY *LASHED* FROM HER AX WITH A *FURIOUS* ATTACK...
"...WHIPS AND CHAINS OF DISHARMONIC *MELODY* WRAPPING ME IN THEIR FIERCE *EMBRACE*...
"...AND I WAS *TRANSFORMED* FROM BEGUILED *BEBOPPER* TO SUPPLICANT *SLAVE*...
"...IN COMPLETE *THRALL* TO THE DEMON *RHYTHMS* OF MODERN JAZZ..."

...AND THE NEXT THING I KNEW, I WAS BEING HAULED IN FOR BREAKING INTO ABSALOM & STREICH.
IT WOULD SEEM THAT SOMEHOW CIRCE HAS BEWITCHED ME.
"THE LADY IS A TRAMP," MAYBE--
--OR "LADY BE GOOD"...
SKSKSKSKSS SKSKSKSKSS
SKSKSKSKSS SKSKSKSKSS
NOT TO WORRY, AL...
...WITH A LITTLE HELP FROM THE AMERICAN SONGBOOK, WE'RE GOING TO WORK A LITTLE HYPNOTIC MAGIC OF OUR OWN ON THIS SIREN.
I'M DROPPING INTO BOP 'TIL YOU DROP CITY THIS EVENING--
--TO FIND OUT JUST WHAT CIRCE O'SHAUGHNESSY IS UP TO.
BUT, TOM-- YOU'RE A MOLDY FIG!
THEN I'LL JUST HAVE TO PUT MY OWN GOOD TASTE ON HOLD FOR THE EVENING, NOW, WON'T I...?
...THAT'S WHAT FRIENDS ARE FOR.
MOLDY FIG?
I'M CERTAIN BIG AL WILL EXPLAIN...

"...IN ENDLESS, PEDANTIC DETAIL."
EMPIRE CITY IS HOME TO MANY BOULEVARDS, THOROUGHFARES, AND RIALTOS--NONE AS WORLD-RENOWNED AS TEMPO STREET.
BLUE SPOT
THE DIAMOND CLUB
MONK'S
TEMPO IS A MERE TWO BLOCKS LONG...
...BUT EVERY NIGHT, FROM DUSK'TIL DAWN, THOSE TWO BLOCKS ARE THE MECCA OF MODERN JAZZ...
...WHERE EVEN A "MOLDY FIG"...
OR "TRADITIONAL JAZZ FAN," TO THOSE IN THE KNOW...
...CAN OCCASIONALLY DIG THOSE CRAZY MODERN SOUNDS TO FIND HIMSELF SOLIDLY SENT, JACKSON.
MUCH AS I HATE TO ADMIT IT, THIS WOMAN IS A SPECTACULAR MUSICIAN...
...BUT THERE'S NOTHING ABOUT HER PLAYING THAT SEEMS EVEN VAGUELY HYPNOTIC.

ON THE OTHER HAND...
..I COULD BE WRO...
...
IN AN INSTANT, TOM'S FREE WILL IS SNATCHED AWAY, WHILE BURIED DEEP WITHIN HIM, A TINY VOICE SHOUTS...
I SHOULDN'T DO THIS...
...BUT I CAN'T STOP MYSELF...
"DADDY WAS A LEPRECHAUN FROM COUNTY KILDARE...
"...MAMA WAS A VOODOO QUEEN FROM OUT OF THE BAYOU..."

...SO I GUESS YOU COULD SAY I'M PURELY BLACK IRISH...
...AND I COME BY MY GIFTS NATURALLY...
...FROM BOTH SIDES O' THE FAMILY.
!!???!??!
--WELL I'LL BE DAMNED IF I DIDN'T CATCH ME A LIVE ONE, NOW--
--WHO'DA GUESSED THIS SWEET BOY--
--WOULD TURN OUT TO BE THE ESCAPIST?
HEY, FELLA-- NOT THAT Y'AIN'T CUTE AN' ALL--
--BUT LET'S NOT GET THE WRONG IDEA--
--LEASTWAYS AS FAR AS HE-IN'-AND-SHE-IN' IS CONCERNED.
AND WHO BETTER'N THE GREATEST ESCAPE ARTIST ALIVE...

"...TO BREAK INTO THE TIGHTEST BANK VAULT IN EMPIRE CITY...
"...AND HAND ME THE PROCEEDS?"
THE ESCAPIST IS TORMENTED, COMPLETELY AWARE OF HIS EVERY MOVE...
THE DE
EMPIRE CITY NATIONAL BANK
...WHILE HE REMAINS UTTERLY HELPLESS IN CIRCE'S SIREN'S PSYCHIC GRASP.
THE ESCAPIST IS A PUPPET, A CLEF NOTE DANGLING FROM THE BARS OF CIRCE'S MUSICAL MADNESS...
...AS THE SINISTER SIREN OF MODERN SOUND WORKS HER IMPROVISATORY WAY THROUGH A SERIES OF MUSICAL QUOTATIONS...
...SAMPLING FROM POP SONGS, SHOW TUNES, AND BALLADS OF THE DAY...
... FROM "SLOW BOAT TO CHINA" TO "WHITE CHRISTMAS" TO "BUTTONS AND BOWS"...

...MUSICAL DOTS CONNECTED BY THE LINES OF HER IMPROVISATIONAL GENIUS...
..."EASY TO LOVE" SEGUES INTO "BYE-BYE BLACKBIRD," THEN "GAL IN CALICO"...
...UNTIL FINALLY, CIRCE MAKES HER FIRST--AND LAST--MISTAKE...
SOONER OR LATER...
...THEY ALL GET TO "I'VE GOT RHYTHM."
AND THANKS TO MY POSTHYPNOTIC SUGGESTION FROM PLUM BLOSSOM...
...I'M MY OLD MOLDY FIG SELF AGAIN.

HEY--
--GETCHERSELF BACK THERE AND GET BACK TO WORK.
SAVE YOUR BREATH, CIRCE--
--MY MIND IS A LOCKED DOOR TO YOU AND YOUR SIREN SONG.
BUT HOW?
SOMETIMES A KEY TAKES THE ODDEST FORM...
...IN THIS CASE, A POSTHYPNOTIC SUGGESTION TO SNAP OUT OF IT THE MINUTE YOU QUOTED "I'VE GOT RHYTHM"--
--AS EVERY BEBOP SAXOPHONIST EVENTUALLY WILL.
NOW IF ONLY YOU'D BEEN A TAD MORE CREATIVE, YOU MIGHT'VE GOTTEN AWAY WITH IT.
MEBBE SO--

BUT I KNOW WHO YOU REALLY ARE BEHIND THAT MASK--
--AND I'LL TELL THE WHOLE WORLD YOUR SECRET.
SOMEHOW, I DON'T THINK SO...
THE SONG MAY BE OVER...
...BUT THE MELODY LINGERS ON.
WHO ARE YOU, CUTIE PIE?
WITH A SINGLE SONIC BLAST, THE ESCAPIST USES CIRCE'S MAGICAL SAXOPHONE TO WIPE HER MEMORY OF THEIR ENCOUNTER CLEAN.

AN' WHO'RE YOU S'POSED TO BE, LADY?
MY NAME IS CIRCE O'SHAUGHNESSY AND I'M HERE TO TURN MYSELF IN...
...WITH A LIST OF THE INNOCENT MEN AND WOMEN I'VE PSYCHICALLY MANIPULATED INTO SERVING AS MY UNWITTING ACCOMPLICES.
WELL, I DUNNO ABOUT THAT...
...BUT I DO KNOW WE GOT A SUITE AT THE RUBBER ROOM HOTEL ALL MADE UP FOR YA, HONEYBUNCH.
AND I KNOW THERE'S SOMETHING ELSE--
--IF I COULD JUST PUT MY FINGER ON IT...
I'M SURE DR. KRONKEIT'LL BE GLAD T'GIVE YA A HAND IN DAT REGARD.

ONLY A FEW BLOCKS AWAY FROM THE 87TH PRECINCT SITS A 19TH-CENTURY BROWNSTONE...
...ONLY BLOCKS AWAY, BUT WORLDS AWAY IN SENSE AND SENSIBILITY.
MUST YOU, YOUNG MASTER?
I COULDN'T AGREE MORE.
SORRY...
BUT ONE OF THE UNFORESEEN RESULTS OF THIS MISADVENTURE...
...IS A NEWFOUND AND GENUINE APPRECIATION FOR THE MODERN SOUND.
WHO COULD'VE GUESSED?
OH, DEAR...
"OH, DEAR," INDEED, MISS PLUM BLOSSOM...
...NOW WE HAVE TWO OF THESE MODERNISTS IN THE HOUSE--AND THIS DISCORDANCE WILL BE A DAILY AFFAIR.
"OH, DEAR," INDEED.
FORGET ABOUT MODERN JAZZ, DADDY-O--
--BIG AL'S HERE TO SAY--
LONG LIVE ROCK-'N'-ROLL!

THE INDY ESCAPIST

by Bubbles LaTour

IN 2002, AFTER A COUPLE YEARS OF PRODUCING MINICOMICS, JEFFREY Brown published his first graphic novel, *Clumsy* — the cartoonist's painful yet often poetic tale of bittersweet young love. This auspicious debut received acclaim both from within the comics community and from without, even earning the indy comics *wunderkind* a spot on National Public Radio.

Clumsy was followed by *Unlikely,* another autobiographical tour de force. And while Brown continues to plumb the depths of narrative nonfiction, often in excruciating detail, it would be a mistake to assume that he shares the disdain of his alt-comics *confrères* for adventure storytelling and, in particular, the superhero genre.

The recent retrospective of Brown's *Early Works,* in fact, lays bare the artist's love of all standard *boy* things: giant monsters; transforming robots; spaceships, guns, and war; and, of course, costumed heroes. As a child of the '80s, the young Jeffrey grew up reading — and loving — Arthur Adams's work on *X-Men.* Brown was also heavily influenced by artist John Romita, Jr., though even the most astute comics critic would be hard-pressed to divine the connection between JR Junior's slick, dynamic line and Brown's intentionally crude drawing style! Though primarily a Marvel Comics fan, Brown faithfully followed Romita, Jr.'s fabled run on *New Adventures of the Escapist* and even had a fan letter printed in issue #9.

Like many adolescents, Brown abandoned comics in favor of more sophisticated, hormonal pursuits — the frustration of which led to his romance with autobiographical stories. In turn, these personal examinations of his own life led back to his childhood and the comics he loved then. This resulted in the superhero spoof *Bighead,* a series of minicomics begun in 2002 and collected in graphic novel form by Top Shelf Productions in 2004.

Although Brown is pretty firmly entrenched in the school of creator ownership, mere conventions of U.S. copyright law cannot keep an artist from his muse, and 2004 also saw the small-press release of two more Brown-penned minis, each starring a boyhood hero of the author's: Wolverine and Escapist.

While Marvel hasn't yet caught on to the quasi-legal* publication of Brown's *Wolverine* minicomic, Dark Horse's legal counsel, prompted by the ever-diligent Harris M. Miller, attorney to the stars, was quick to fire off a cease-and-desist letter to Brown, threatening to file a major lawsuit claiming copyright infringement should he continue his unauthorized publication and distribution of *Escapist* comics. The editor of this magazine, however, was so charmed by Brown's mini that she brokered a deal with the cartoonist to print his story, rather than take him to court. Brown graciously agreed.

---

* In defense of the artist, it should be noted that Brown received no money for either his *Wolverine* or his *Escapist* mini, instead handing them out for free to friends and acquaintances.

THE ESCAPIST ESCAPES AGAIN!

SHORTLY...
HELLOOOO, ESCAPIST.

HE'S SEMI-CONSCIOUS, BUT COMPLETELY IMMOBILE.
POKE
POKE

ONE MORE INJECTION AND HE'LL BE READY...

MY MASTERPIECE IS FINALLY READY. IT TOOK TEN YEARS AND MILLIONS OF DOLLARS IN GOVERNMENT GRANTS, VERY LITTLE OF WHICH I SPENT ON EATING OUT OR BUYING ELECTRONIC EQUIPMENT FOR PERSONAL USE.

IN A FEW MINUTES, THE COMPUTER WILL BEGIN ANALYZING THE ESCAPIST'S BRAIN ACTIVITY -- IN ESSENCE, READING HIS MIND!
TAK
TAK
TAK

SOON, ALL THE SECRETS OF THE ESCAPIST AND THE LEAGUE OF THE GOLDEN KEY WILL BE REVEALED TO ME! HA!

ESCAPIST, EVEN THOUGH WE JUST MET, I THINK I... I LOVE YOU...

YOU'RE SO SMART AND HANDSOME. I CAN'T BELIEVE YOU'RE SINGLE...

PERHAPS I'VE BEEN WAITING FOR A SPECIAL WOMAN... A WOMAN LIKE YOU...
OH... OH, ESCAPIST...

MMM MMPH MM MMM MPH MM

I DON'T UNDERSTAND... THESE AREN'T SECRETS. THIS IS SOME IMAGINARY SOAP OPERA!
I GUESS IT'S 'CAUSE I ASKED HIM ABOUT HAVING A GIRLFRIEND.

WHAT?! FOOL WOMAN! THE MACHINE READS WHATEVER THOUGHTS ARE PRESENT WHEN THE SUBJECT IS RENDERED UNCONSCIOUS!

YOU ASK THE ESCAPIST ABOUT HIS SECRETS, AND THEN HE CAN'T HELP BUT THINK ABOUT THEM, AND THEN YOU HIT HIM WITH THE KNOCKOUT GAS

OH. WELL, YOU NEVER TOLD ME THAT.

YES I DID!
NO, I WOULD'VE REMEMBERED.

I DID TELL YOU.
NO YOU DIDN'T.
YES I DID.
YOU DIDN'T.
I DID TOO.
NUNH-UNH.

WELL, I THOUGHT I DID.
WELL, YOU DIDN'T.

OUR ONLY CHANCE IS TO INJECT MORE SERUM.
WON'T THAT KILL HIM?

PROBABLY. BUT IT'S OUR ONLY CHANCE TO REVEAL DEEPER MEMORIES THAT WILL SHOW US HOW TO DEFEAT THE LEAGUE OF THE GOLDEN KEY.

THE ESCAPIST WAS GOOD TO ME... IT'D BE A SHAME TO KILL HIM...
SQUIRT
SQUIRT
EMPTY

IT'S WORKING... I THINK IT'S WORKING... SOON THE SECRETS WILL BE REVEALED...
TAK
TAK
TAK
TAK

OH, ESCAPIST, YOU'RE SO WONDERFUL.

WELL, I GUESS WE'LL JUST HAVE TO KILL HIM.
CLICK
CLACK

WAIT! UM, I'VE GOT A BETTER IDEA...

WHAT IF WE STAGE A FAILED ATTEMPT AT AN ESCAPE? WE COULD MAKE IT LOOK LIKE THE ESCAPIST WAS DRUNK AND COULDN'T GET OUT OF A SIMPLE TRAP...

THE POSTER BOY FOR THE LEAGUE OF THE GOLDEN KEY WILL BE EXPOSED AS A FAKE, AND THE LEAGUE WILL BE SHAMED...

HMMM... IT'S IMPROBABLE AND CONVOLUTED, BUT FOR SOME REASON I FIND IT VERY APPEALING...

SO...
HE'S PARALYZED FROM THE SERUM, SO WE CAN JUST LEAVE HIM HERE TO DROWN.

OOH, LET'S GO GET MY NEW DIGITAL CAMERA!
CLAP
CLAP
CLAP
CLAP
CLAP
CLAP

HOWEVER, JUST AS THE ESCAPIST IS ABOUT TO DROWN IN THE SLOWLY FILLING BATHTUB, A SUDDEN, BARELY PERCEPTIBLE CHANGE COMES OVER HIS EYES...

IT LOOKS LIKE THE SERUM HAS WORN OFF! MAYBE SHE HAD FEELINGS FOR ME AFTER ALL...

JUST HAVE TO GET OUT OF THESE ROPES...ERM...

THE WINDOW IS BRICKED OVER AND THE AIR VENT IS BLOCKED... I'LL HAVE TO BREAK DOWN THE DOOR.

BANG!

OH, THAT DOOR WAS UNLOCKED...

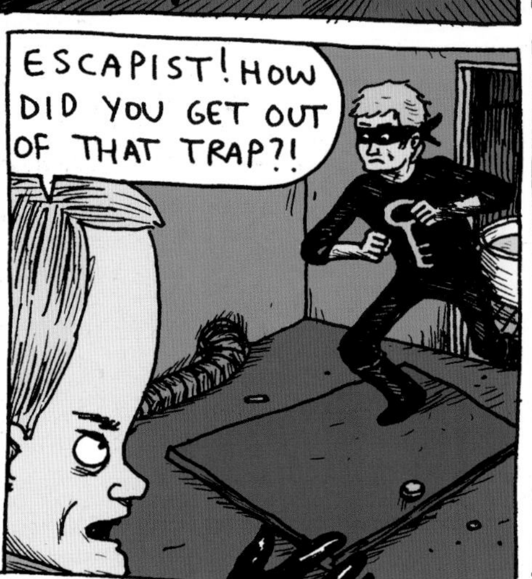
ESCAPIST! HOW DID YOU GET OUT OF THAT TRAP?!
IF ONLY MY MACHINE HAD WORKED, I'D KNOW. NO MATTER, I'LL DEFEAT YOU WITH MY BARE HANDS—WHICH HAPPEN TO BE HOLDING THIS IRON BAR...

FWISH!
ENH!
ENH!

POW!

OH, ESCAPIST... I'M SORRY I TRICKED YOU. I... I REALLY DID CARE ABOUT YOU.

I GUESS SOMETIMES SOME THINGS JUST AREN'T MEANT TO BE. I HAVE TO TIE YOU UP UNTIL THE POLICE GET HERE.

I... UNDERSTAND.

SO, ESCAPIST... I MAY NOT HAVE LEARNED YOUR SECRETS OF ESCAPING, BUT I DID LEARN ONE SECRET...

... THE SECRET OF YOUR HEART!

PERHAPS... BUT HEARTS CHANGE. NOW I'M SINGLE, AND FREE ONCE AGAIN!

WHEN WILL THE IRON CHAIN LEARN—YOU CAN'T ESCAPE FROM FREEDOM!

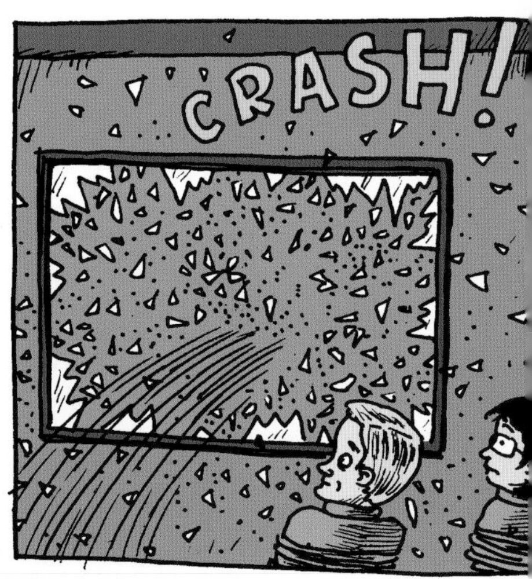
CRASH!

OH, YEAH? WELL... WELL, YOU CAN'T ESCAPE FROM BEING THE ESCAPIST!

UM, I THINK HE'S GONE ALREADY.

WE SHOULD'VE TAKEN OFF HIS MASK FIRST TO SEE WHO HE WAS.
YEAH.
FIN

“THE FINAL CURTAIN”

PREFACE
by Jason Hall

Exactly what four-color moment the Silver Age of comic books ended on is one of those classically heated ongoing discussions among comics fandom — right up there with the question: “Who’s faster, Superman or the Flash?” However, with the fortuitous and fortunate discovery of “The Final Curtain,” it’s now safe to say that the dropping of said curtain on the Silver Age came a tad early for the Escapist.

Comics have always been socially (and therefore, one could argue, morally) relevant to some degree. The Golden Age was strewn with pro-American, anti-Axis messages, at least as far back as *All-Star Comics* #4 (March-April 1941) wherein J. Edgar Hoover sent the Justice Society on a mission to thwart the efforts of the “Grey-Shirts” — a Hitlerian, Bund-like organization preaching the benefits of a totalitarian government. Sure, they weren’t *called* Nazis — but there wasn’t an American who couldn’t read between those very wide lines (not that readers had to for long — by issue #9, the JSA were battling the minions of “Hitler and the Fascists”). Behind the punches thrown by the likes of Hourman, Green Lantern, and the Sandman, readers were presented a clear message: the Nazis are bad. Simple and true — and a definitive social/moral stance.

But it was the death of the Silver Age that gave birth to comic book tales most notably considered today as “relevant.” While pages were still bursting with action, stories became more realistic, dealing with many of the prevalent issues (drugs, racism, equality, war, the environment) of the late 1960s. Many comics historians look to the infamous O’Neil/Adams Green Lantern/Green Arrow teaming (beginning with *Green Lantern* #76, April 1970), 29 years after the aforementioned *All-Star Comics* #4, as the start of a socially conscious cynicism taking the forefront in comics. However, when one considers “The Final Curtain,” as one must, it’s the Escapist that takes the gold. (Or perhaps, more appropriately, the *bronze*, as even the story’s title works not only as a symbol of its controversial topic of euthanasia, but in hindsight also as a historical representation of bringing the Silver Age to a close and raising the curtain on the Bronze Age of comic book history.)

“The Final Curtain” was written and drawn sometime in 1968 and was the last story produced by Fab Comics — one of five different publishers churning out competing versions of the Escapist. And it very well may have caused the end of what is now referred to as “The Wild Years” period of *Escapist* history.

A more earnest, and certainly more controversial, story than what was typically being produced during that period, it somehow floated past the proverbial powers-that-be all the way through to the printing press — but the buck (or, more accurately, the paper) stopped there. Before being distributed to the public, a copy of the printed comic found its way under the bulbous nose of Gerald Sunshine, who

Big Al’s hospital stay sets the stage for “The Final Curtain.”

had only just recently secured *all rights* to the Escapist and related characters. And even without an unfortunately named feminine hygiene device or a super-powered baby-in-a-microwave anywhere in sight, the comic was ordered pulped — due, of course, to the sensitive nature of the story's theme concerning euthanasia. Immediately after this fiasco, Gerald Sunshine ceased publication of all *Escapist* comics.

Coincidence? Perhaps.

The argument for euthanasia. Too daring for 1968 — *and* for Gerald Sunshine.

The publicly stated reason was his supposed greater interest in pursuing television, film, and theme park endeavors. However, the true *raison d'être* is purported to be that Sunshine's father had suffered an agonizingly drawn-out death from cancer just six months prior. Apparently, perhaps due to feelings of guilt, this story rubbed the new owner of the Escapist the wrong way.

As a result, copies of this story have become the "holy grail" of comic book connoisseurs, with only four copies rumored to have surfaced so far (one said to have garnered an ungodly amount of money in private auction). Of course, this is all merely urban legend. But we do know that at least one copy survived (perhaps the copy Gerald Sunshine read himself, kept for sentimental reasons?), because it wound up in the hands of Gerald's son, Danny Sonnenschein. A lifelong fan of the Escapist, Danny was bequeathed control of the Sunshine Media Group upon his father's death (also of cancer) — and thus began the "Sunshine Comics" era of the Escapist. As comics historians know, stories from this period attempted to present the character as more "relevant" and "gritty" — an inspiration, one might surmise, taken from Danny's reading of "The Final Curtain."

On a semi-related side note, the one-page Golden Age flashback used in this story is an actual page of art from a never published (and never completed!) story from the early 1940s: the reason involving a sordid office love triangle, a band of gypsies, and an odd addiction to ink fumes. But that's a story for another time ...

So now, as the lights go down, sit back and enjoy for the first time in official print ... "The Final Curtain."

(Oh, and by the way, the Flash would beat Superman *hands down*.)

A precursor to the era of "relevant" comics, "The Final Curtain" did not shy away from the gruesome nature of its topic.

the final curtain

OUR LADY OF ETERNAL PEACE, EMPIRE CITY.
THANK YOU FOR THE VISIT, MY BOY...
Emerge

OUR MISSION SEEMS TO GET MORE DANGEROUS BY THE DAY.
I MUST ADMIT, I FEEL A BIT LIKE SOME MAD SCULPTOR'S ABSURD GALLERY PIECE.
BUT A PRICELESS ONE, AL. BALL 'N' CHAIN IS SAFELY LOCKED BEHIND BARS, THANKS TO YOU.

YES... THOUGH I HAVE A FEELING THIS WOUND WILL BE NAGGING ME FOR QUITE SOME TIME.
I'M SURPRISED THEY HAVEN'T NAMED A WING HERE AFTER US YET.
I'M SORRY, MR. ESCAPIST, BUT VISITING TIME IS OVER.

AH, MY DEAR... TIME FOR ANOTHER SPONGE BATH, PERHAPS?
GIGGLE OH, AREN'T YOU QUITE THE HANDFUL!
TAKE GOOD CARE OF HIM, MISS--

-- JUST DON'T LET HIM SHOW YOU WHY HE'S CALLED "BIG AL"!

I'VE ALWAYS HATED BEING IN HOSPITALS. THEIR PURPOSE IS TO HEAL-- TO FREE US FROM PAIN AND SUFFERING...
UNNHH...

...YET, TO ME, THEY ALWAYS FEEL LIKE A PRISON.

YOU'RE CONFINED IN A SMALL, NONDESCRIPT ROOM, TWENTY-FOUR HOURS A DAY-- EXCEPT FOR PERHAPS THE RARE WALK DOWN THE HALL, CLOSELY GUARDED BY A NURSE.
EXCUSE ME, SIR.
IS HE OKAY? WHAT'S WRONG WITH HIM?
TERMINAL CANCER. THERE'S NOT MUCH THE DOCTORS CAN DO FOR HIM... EXCEPT KEEP HIM ALIVE.
UGH...
ONE BARELY EDIBLE CAFETERIA MEAL AFTER ANOTHER, PUMPED-IN AIR--

IT'S WORSE WHEN THE MORPHINE WEARS OFF. A TERRIBLE WAY TO GO.
AGH--* OHHH...
DOES THE MAN HAVE ANY FAMILY? ANYONE AT ALL?
NO-- THERE'S NO ONE. BUT THAT'S HOW IT IS FOR ALL OF US, REALLY, AT THE VERY END.

--COMPLETELY ISOLATED FROM THE OUTSIDE WORLD.
AND VISITING TIME IS OVER-- EVEN FOR "SUPERHEROES"! OR WHATEVER.

OR PERHAPS IT ISN'T JUST THE HOSPITAL--
...PLEASE...

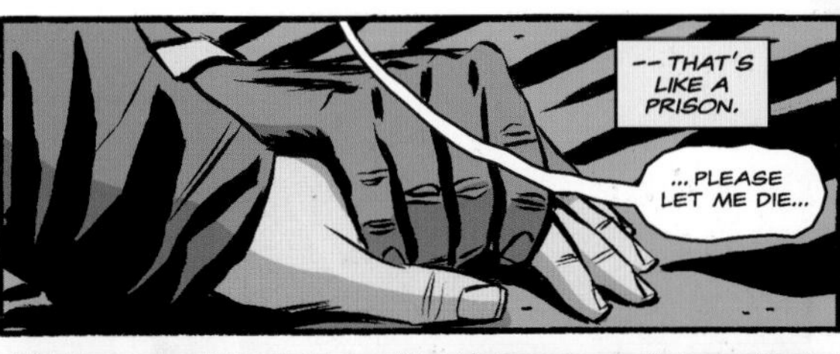
--THAT'S LIKE A PRISON.
...PLEASE LET ME DIE...

THE IMPRISONIST CAPTURED ME WAY TOO EASILY. MY HEAD WASN'T IN THE GAME.
SNAP
MY THOUGHTS WERE STILL BACK IN THAT STERILE ROOM WITH THE OLD MAN.

AND AS I ESCAPED...

...GASPING AND GRASPING FOR LIFE...

GASP!
...I COULD SEE ONLY HIS FRAIL FORM PLEADING FOR DEATH.

TO SAY I WAS DISTRACTED OVER THE FOLLOWING WEEK IS PUTTING IT MILDLY...

HERE I AM, SOMEONE WHOSE VERY EXISTENCE IS DEFINED BY MY MISSION TO LIBERATE ALL THOSE WHO TOIL IN OPPRESSION OF ANY KIND...

TO PROMOTE EMBRACING A LIFE OF FREEDOM, NOT TOSSING IT AWAY...
YET, THIS MAN WAS PLAGUED BY LIFE ITSELF-- A LIFE SOMEHOW SLOWLY TRANSFORMED INTO A VILE PRISON, SHACKLED BY DISEASE.
The Quick Escape

I HAD NO CHOICE BUT TO HELP--

--EVEN IF IT WERE TO FREE HIM ONLY MOMENTARILY OF HIS PRISON.

HOW CAN THE ESCAPIST POSSIBLY DODGE HIS OWN DOOMED FATE AT THE FATAL TOUCH OF... THE REAPER?!

R.I.P.
The ESCAPIST
THUNK

I'LL ADD "HIT AND RUN" TO YOUR LAUNDRY LIST OF LARCENIES, REAPER!
ROOM

WHOA!
SCREECH!

THUD
OOOF--
NOW FEEL THE ICY HAND OF DEATH IN THE GUISE OF COLD, HARD STEEL!

-- AND REFLECTED IN HIS LIFELESS EYES, I COULD SEE NOTHING BUT MY OWN ILL-FATED DEMISE...

NOW, HOW THE HELL'D YOU MANAGE TO GET OUTTA THAT ONE?!
I'D BEEN VISITING LEWIS EVERY DAY FOR THE PAST WEEK, HOPING THE TALES OF MY ADVENTURES WOULD SOMEHOW RAISE THE MAN'S SPIRITS...

AND IT SEEMED TO BE WORKING--
I'LL TELL YOU TOMORROW.

--THOUGH TALES OF FOLLY AND FISTICUFFS WERE A FAR CRY FROM ACTUAL THERAPY. I WISHED THERE WERE SOMETHING MORE I COULD DO FOR THE OLD GUY.
IT'S FUNNY, BUT... UNGH... BUT FOR ME, YOUR STORY IS WHAT THEM FANCY WRITERS WOULD CALL IRONIC.
YOU WERE DOIN' YOUR BEST TO RUN FROM DEATH...

...AND HERE I AM, WANTIN' NOTHIN' MORE THAN TO WELCOME IT LIKE AN OLD FRIEND.

YOU KNOW, I TOOK MY GAL VIOLET TO SEE YOUR MISTER MISTERIOSO AT THE EMPIRE BACK IN THE DAY...
MAN, WHAT A SHOW!
BOWL of FIRE club
"AFTERWARDS, WE DECIDED TO TOP THE EVENING OFF WITH A BIT OF RUG-CUTTIN'."
I... I WAS GONNA ASK HER TO BE MY WIFE THAT NIGHT...
"BUT I NEVER GOT THE CHANCE..."
HANDS OFF THE WHEEL!
BOWL of FIRE club

SMASH!
ONCE SHE WAS GONE, I WAS ALL ALONE... NEVER FOUND NOBODY ELSE... NEVER WANTED TO.
ALWAYS WONDERED IF MY HEART BREAKIN' WAS SOMEHOW THE CAUSE OF MY ILLNESS.

DOCTORS CAN'T PROVE THAT SORTA THING... BUT I KNOW I STARTED DYIN' THE DAY SHE WAS TAKEN AWAY FROM ME.

AN' ALL I GOT LEFT IS THE PAIN.
I'VE HAD A GOOD LIFE, AT LEAST WHILE MY GAL WAS PART OF IT. BUT I'M READY TO GO ON. AND THESE DAMN DOCTORS WON'T LET ME!
THEY'RE HOLDING ME PRISONER IN THIS WORLD WITH THEIR NEEDLES AND THEIR DOPE. IT AIN'T NATURAL!

YOU'RE THE ESCAPIST! AIN'T YA SUPPOSED TO HELP PEOPLE ESCAPE?
I'M TRAPPED HERE, SON. I JUST WANNA BE SET FREE. I--

JUST RELAX, MR. WASHINGTON. I'LL TAKE CARE OF THAT.
WUGHHH!

DON'T YOU WORRY.
OOOHH--*

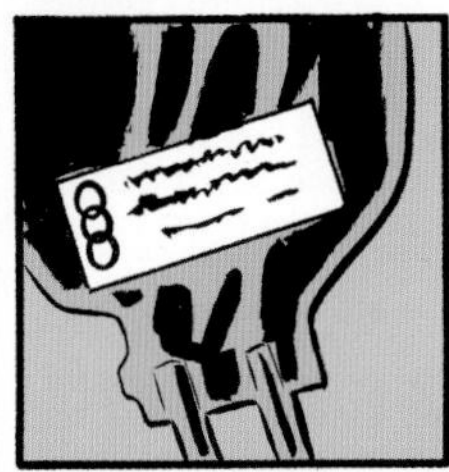

CLICK

GENTLEMEN...

WHAT COMPELS YOU TO CALL UPON THE LEAGUE OF THE GOLDEN KEY, TOM MAYFLOWER?

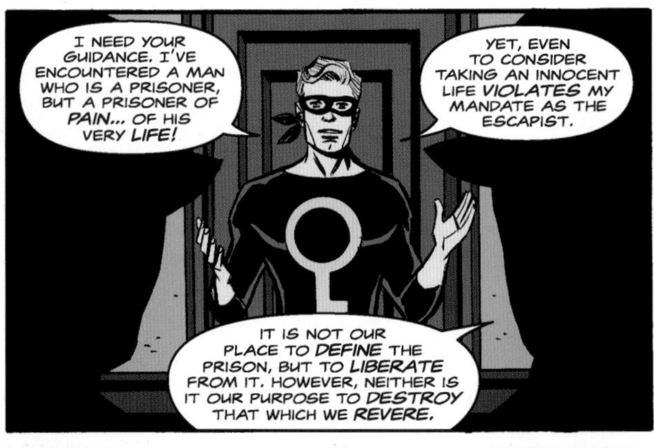
I NEED YOUR GUIDANCE. I'VE ENCOUNTERED A MAN WHO IS A PRISONER, BUT A PRISONER OF PAIN... OF HIS VERY LIFE!
YET, EVEN TO CONSIDER TAKING AN INNOCENT LIFE VIOLATES MY MANDATE AS THE ESCAPIST.
IT IS NOT OUR PLACE TO DEFINE THE PRISON, BUT TO LIBERATE FROM IT. HOWEVER, NEITHER IS IT OUR PURPOSE TO DESTROY THAT WHICH WE REVERE.

I'M SICK OF YOUR DAMN RIDDLES! WHAT DOES THAT MEAN?

"IT MEANS... YOU'RE ON YOUR OWN."

SOMETIMES THE RIGHT DECISION IS CONCEALED FROM US... LIKE A BIT OF MISDIRECTION IN A MAGIC TRICK.
WE'RE DISTRACTED BY WHAT WE'RE LED TO BELIEVE IS RIGHT...

...INSTEAD OF SEEING THE TRUTH BEFORE OUR EYES.

THE TRUTH THAT'S HIDDEN BY OUR FEAR TO ACCEPT IT.

I KNOW I HAVE ONLY ONE CHOICE:

THE RIGHT ONE.
ESCAPIST... THAT YOU...?

YES, LEWIS. AND I'M HERE--

--TO SET YOU FREE.

EXCUSE ME, NURSE, BUT MR. WASHINGTON HAS PASSED ON.

TOP SHELF THEATRE
presents
THE MAGNIFICENT MEPHISTO
WHERE DID LEWIS ESCAPE TO? WHO CAN SAY.
FOR HIM, ESCAPING WASN'T ABOUT WHERE HE WAS GOING. IT WAS JUST ABOUT FREEDOM.

HIS WAS A PRISON OF THE FLESH, AN ORGANIC TORTURE CHAMBER THAT HAD TURNED AGAINST HIM LONG AGO-- FROM WHICH HIS SOUL BEGGED TO BE FREE.
club
HE'S MADE HIS FINAL ESCAPE, THE CURTAIN HAS DROPPED...

...AND I LEAVE MY SEAT IN THE AUDIENCE NOT KNOWING WHERE HIS JOURNEY HAS TAKEN HIM...
...BUT HOPING WHEREVER IT MAY BE...

...THAT HE'S DANCING.

Curtain

COVER GALLERY

A Tantalizing Trio of Colorful Covers
Designed with Dazzling Deliberation
by a Convocation of Crackerjack Creators

Matt Wagner

Will Eisner
with Norm Breyfogle, Eddie Campbell,
Howard Chaykin, Jason, & Thomas Yeates
and designed by Amy Arendts

Bill Morrison

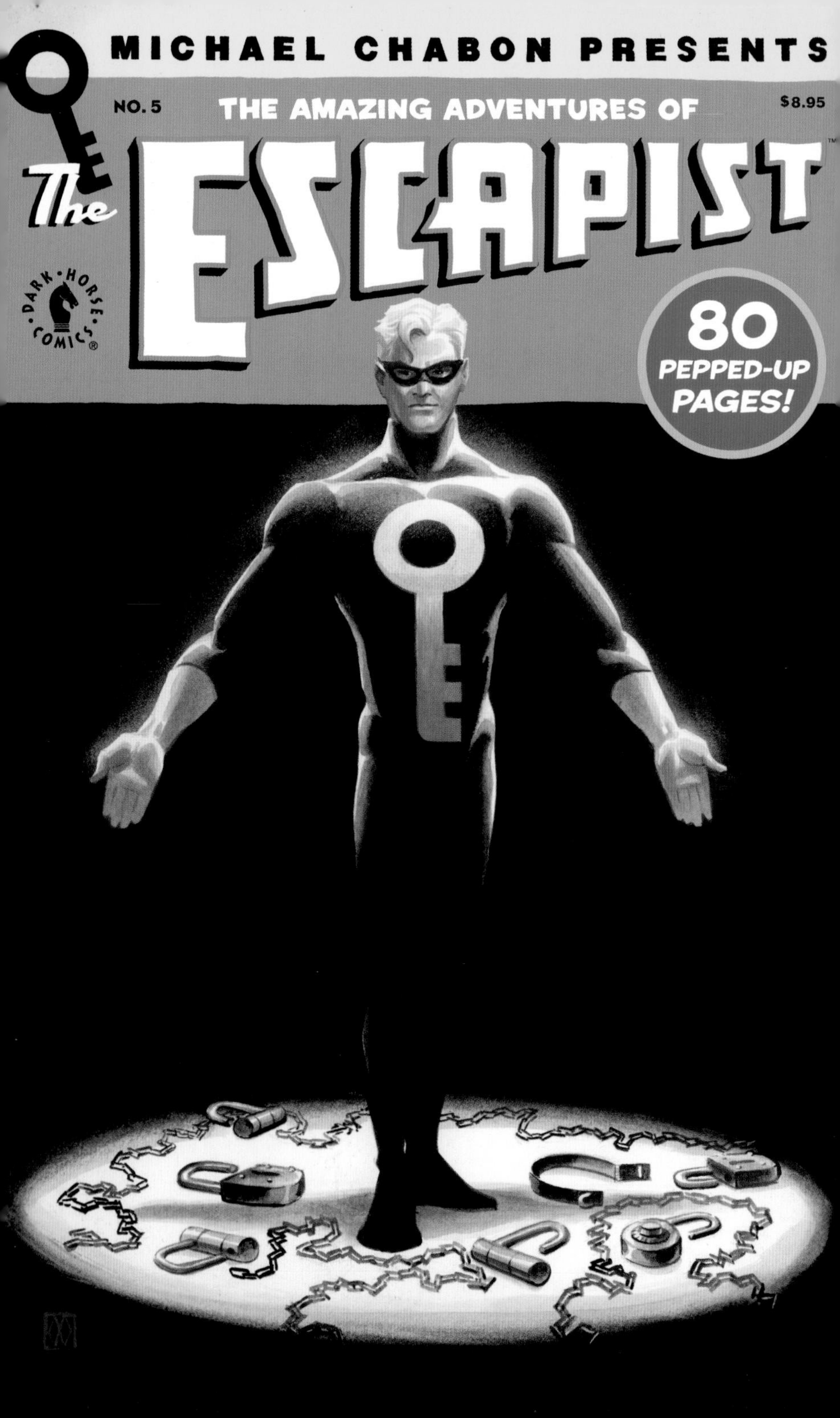
MICHAEL CHABON PRESENTS
NO. 5
THE AMAZING ADVENTURES OF
$8.95
The ESCAPIST™
DARK HORSE COMICS®
80 PEPPED-UP PAGES!